JUMP Math

Book 1 Part 1 of 2

T0302628

Contents

jump math

MULTIPLYING POTENTIAL.

JUMP Math
One Yonge Street, Suite 1014
Toronto, Ontario M5E 1E5
Canada
www.jumpmath.org

Writers: Dr. John Mighton
Consultants: Dr. Anna Klebanov, Dr. Sohrab Rahbar, Dr. Sindi Sabourin
Editors: Megan Burns, Liane Tsui, Natalie Francis, Annie Chern, Julia Cochrane, Janice Dyer, Laura Edlund, Neomi Majmudar, Una Malcolm, Jodi Rauch
Layout and Illustrations: Linh Lam, Gabriella Kerr
Cover Design: Blakeley Words+Pictures
Cover Photograph: © iStockphoto.com/George Bailey

ISBN 978-1-927457-32-0

Fifth printing June 2023

Printed and bound in Canada

Welcome to JUMP Math

Entering the world of JUMP Math means believing that every child has the capacity to be fully numerate and to love math. Founder and mathematician John Mighton has used this premise to develop his innovative teaching method. The resulting resources isolate and describe concepts so clearly and incrementally that everyone can understand them.

JUMP Math is comprised of Teacher Resources, Digital Lesson Slides, student Assessment & Practice Books, assessment tools, outreach programs, and professional development. All of this is presented on the JUMP Math website: **www.jumpmath.org**.

The Teacher Resource is available on the website for free use. Read the introduction to the Teacher Resource before you begin using these materials. This will ensure that you understand both the philosophy and the methodology of JUMP Math. The Assessment & Practice Books are designed for use by students, with adult guidance. Each student will have unique needs and it is important to provide the student with the appropriate support and encouragement as they work through the material.

Allow students to discover the concepts by themselves as much as possible. Mathematical discoveries can be made in small, incremental steps. The discovery of a new step is like untangling the parts of a puzzle. It is exciting and rewarding.

Students will need to answer the questions marked with a in a notebook. Grid paper notebooks should always be on hand for answering extra questions or when additional room for calculation is needed.

Contents

Unit 4: Operations and Algebraic Thinking: Introduction to Subtraction

Unit 5: Measurement and Data: Measuring Length

Unit 6: Operations and Algebraic Thinking: Applying Strategies for Addition and Subtraction

PART 2

Unit 1: Number and Operations in Base Ten: Understanding Place Value

Unit 2: Number and Operations in Base Ten: Using Place Value to Add and Subtract

Unit 3: Operations and Algebraic Thinking: Problem Solving with Pictures, Models, and Equations

Unit 4: Measurement and Data: Telling and Writing Time

Unit 5: Geometry: Reasoning with Shapes

Unit 6: Measurement and Data: Representing and Interpreting Data

OAI-I Counting

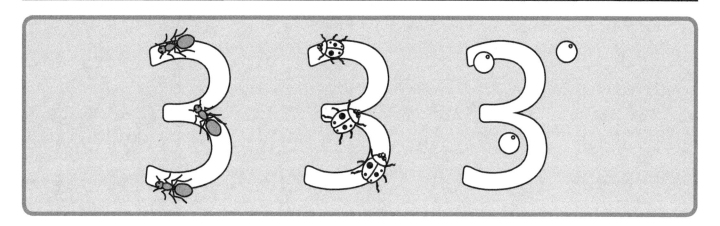

☐ Color.

1.
3 ants

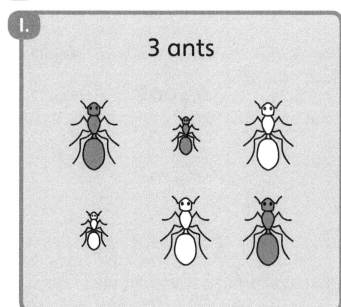

2.
3 ladybugs

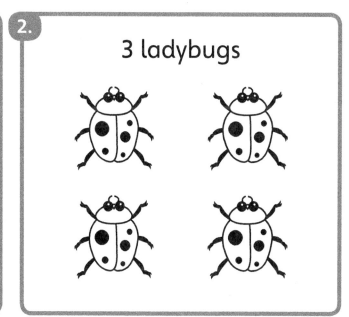

3.
3 bubbles

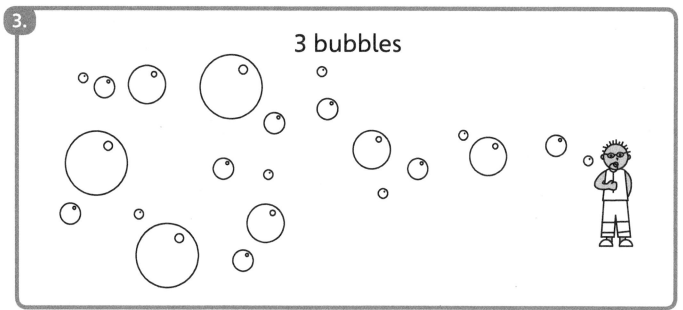

☐ Color.

4. 2 spots

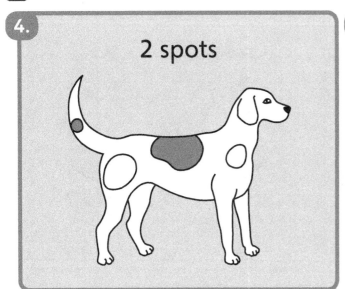

5. 4 spots

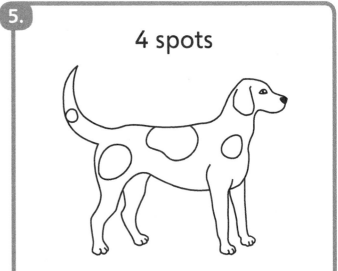

6. 3 spots

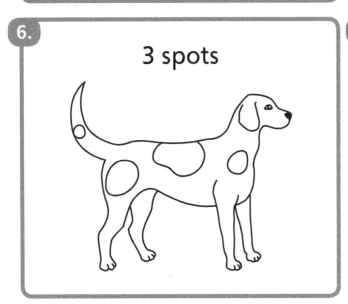

7. I spot

OAI-2 Match by Counting

☐ Match by number.

1.

2.

3.

Match by number.

4.

5.

4

Operations and Algebraic Thinking I-2

☐ Match by number.

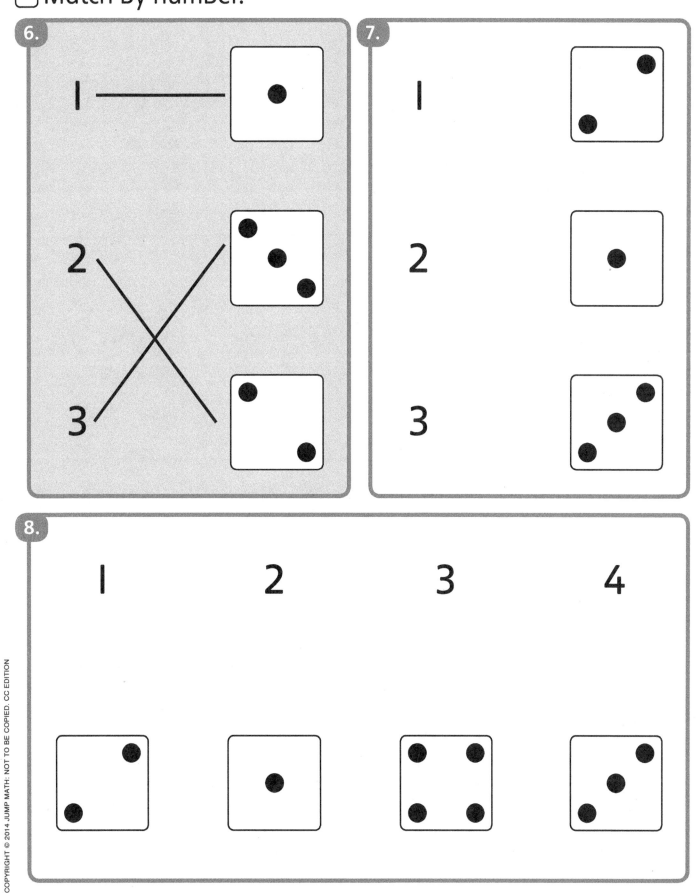

☐ Match by number.

9.

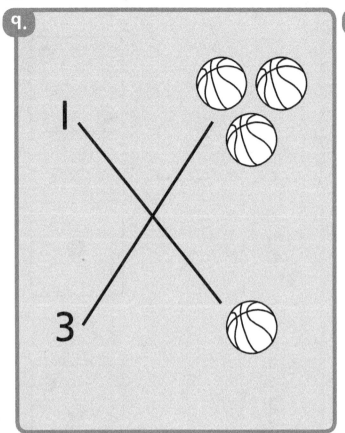

1

3

10.

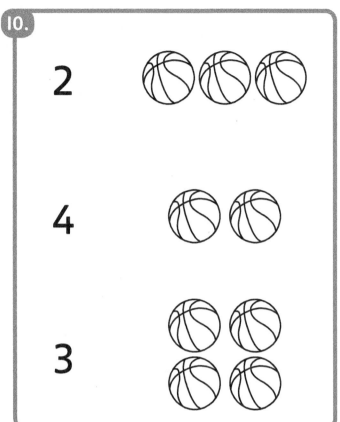

2

4

3

11.

7   9   6   8

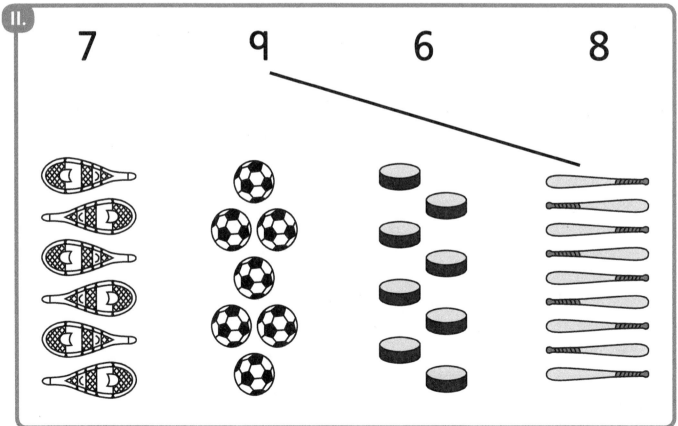

Operations and Algebraic Thinking 1-2

☐ Circle the groups of 5.
☐ Cross out the other groups.

12.
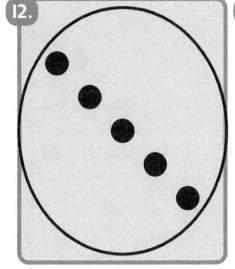

13.

14.

15.

16.
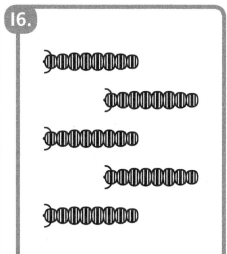

17.
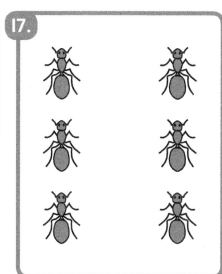

18.

19.
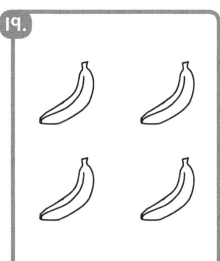

20.
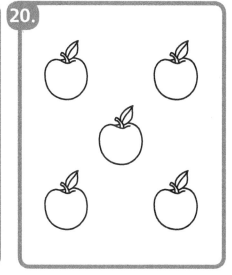

OAI-3 Zero

☐ Match by number.

1.

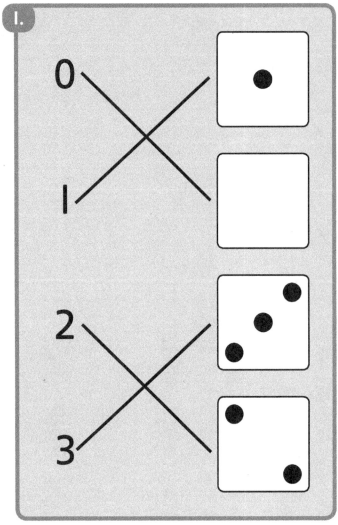

2.

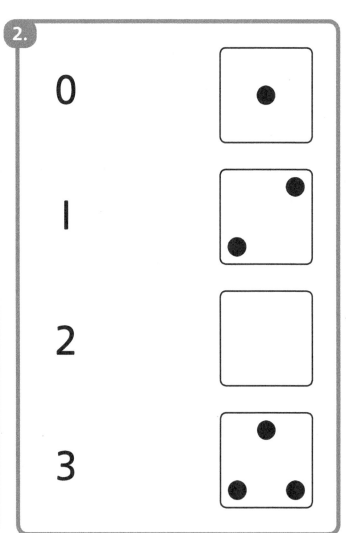

3.

0   1   2   3   4

☐ Match by number.

4.

3

1

0

2

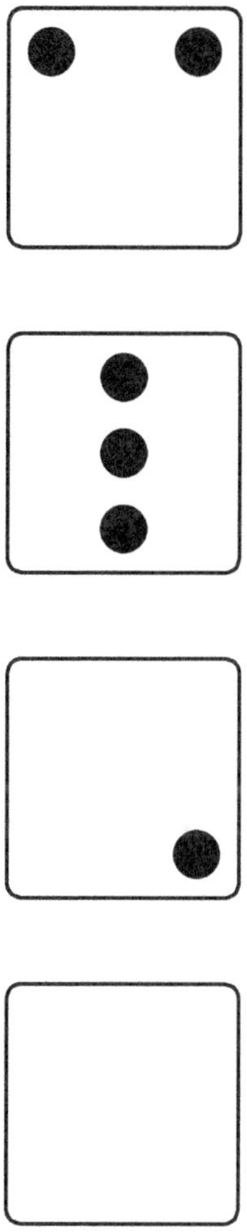

5.

2

3

1

0

6.

3　　1　　4　　0　　2

☐ Circle.

7.
3 frogs

8.
1 penguin

9.
0 grasshoppers

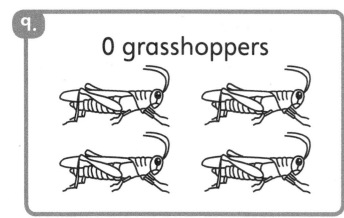

10.
4 bunnies

11.
2 hamsters

12.
3 bears

Operations and Algebraic Thinking 1-3

0 1 2 3 4 5 6 7 8 9

☐ Circle the numbers.

13. (3) Ɛ

14. ʎ 4

15. 5 ट

16. 6 ϱ

17. 8 ∞

18. ɯ 3

19. q d

20. p q

21. 2 ट

22. Γ 7 ∠ ⌐

23. Γ q 8 ʎ

24. BONUS Γ 3 0 ∞ ϱ ट 5 0

OAI-4 Writing Numbers

☐ Join the dots in order.

1.

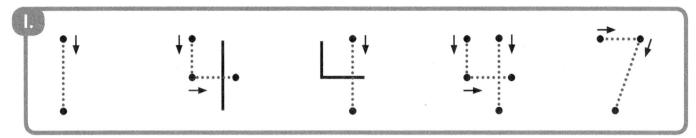

☐ Trace.

2.

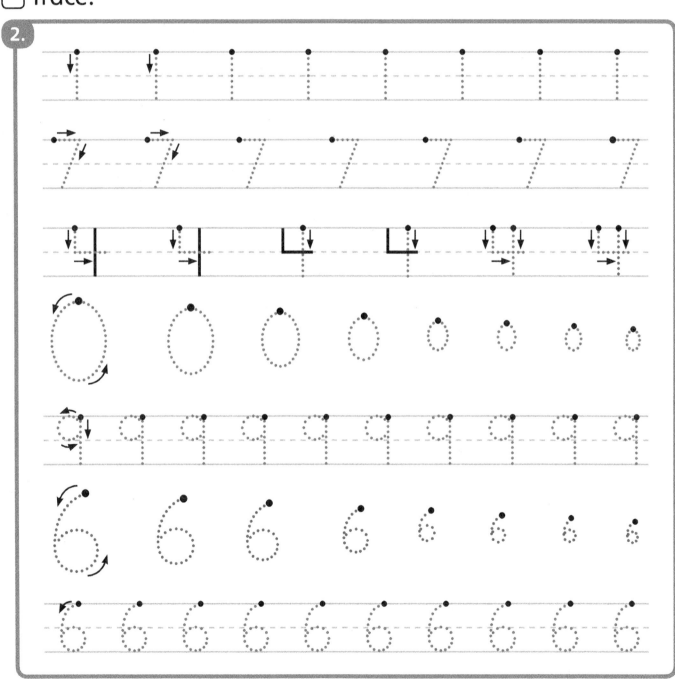

☐ Trace.

3.

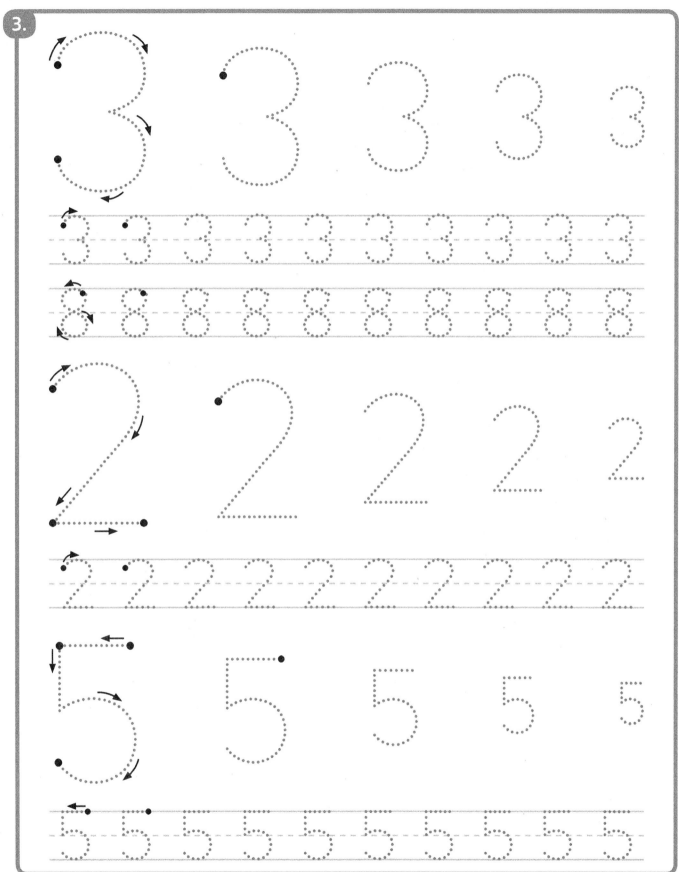

☐ How many legs?

4.

2   4   6   8

5.

2   4   6   8

6.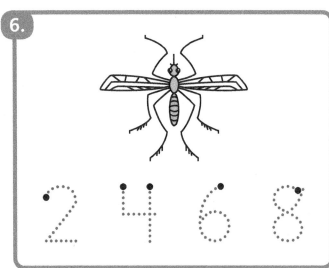

2   4   6   8

7.

2   4   6   8

8.

2   4   6   8

q.

2   4   6   8

☐ **BONUS:** Insects have 6 legs. Circle the insects.

Operations and Algebraic Thinking 1-4

OAI-5 Counting On

☐ Count the puppies.

1.

___5___ puppies

2.

_____ puppies

3.

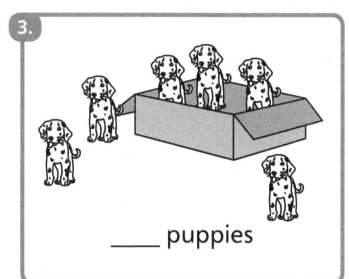

_____ puppies

4.

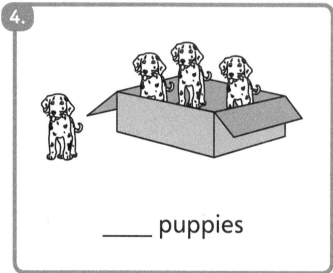

_____ puppies

5.

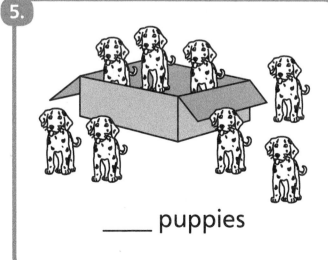

_____ puppies

6.

_____ puppies

☐ Count the fingers that are up.

7.

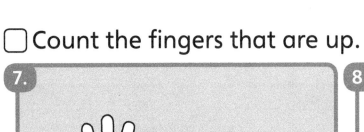

___6___ fingers up

8.

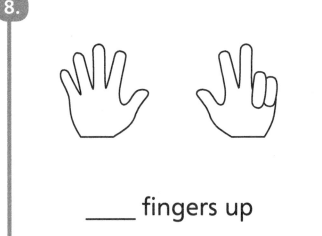

_____ fingers up

9.

_____ fingers up

10.

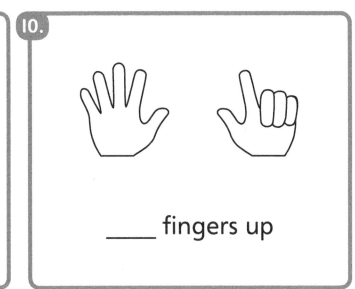

_____ fingers up

11.

_____ fingers up

12.

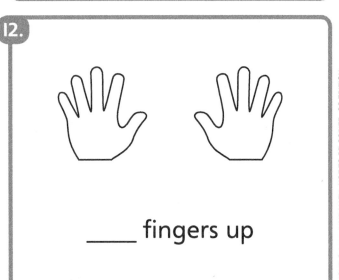

_____ fingers up

Operations and Algebraic Thinking I-5

OAI-6 Counting Using a Chart

☐ Trace the numbers.
☐ How many fish?

1.

There are ___5___ fish.

2.

There are _____ fish.

3.

There are _____ fish.

4.

There are _____ fish.

☐ How many ants?

5.

1 2 3 4 5 6 7 8 9 10

There are ___6___ ants.

6.

1 2 3 4 5 6 7 8 9 10

There are _____ ants.

7.

1 2 3 4 5 6 7 8 9 10

There are _____ ants.

8.

1 2 3 4 5 6 7 8 9 10

There are _____ ants.

Operations and Algebraic Thinking 1-6

☐ How many blocks?

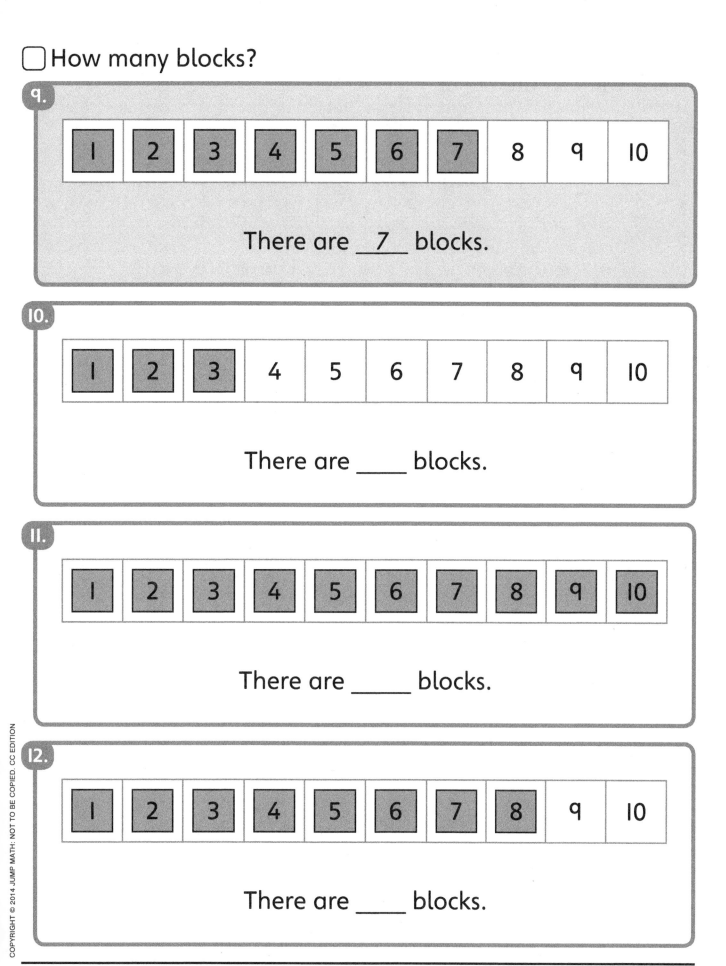

9.

| 1 | 2 | 3 | 4 | 5 | 6 | 7 | 8 | 9 | 10 |

There are __7__ blocks.

10.

| 1 | 2 | 3 | 4 | 5 | 6 | 7 | 8 | 9 | 10 |

There are ____ blocks.

11.

| 1 | 2 | 3 | 4 | 5 | 6 | 7 | 8 | 9 | 10 |

There are ____ blocks.

12.

| 1 | 2 | 3 | 4 | 5 | 6 | 7 | 8 | 9 | 10 |

There are ____ blocks.

OAI-7 More and Fewer

 Are there **more** ☐ or △?

1.

△1 △2

☐1 ☐2 ☐3 ☐4 ☐5

There are more ☐ .

2.

△1 △2 △3 △4 △5

☐1 ☐2 ☐3

There are more ____ .

3.

△1 △2 △3 △4

☐1 ☐2 ☐3 ☐4 ☐5

There are more ____ .

4.

△1 △2 △3

☐1 ☐2 ☐3 ☐4 ☐5

There are more ____ .

5.

△1

☐1 ☐2 ☐3

There are more ____ .

6.

△1 △2 △3 △4 △5

☐1 ☐2 ☐3 ☐4

There are more ____ .

7.

△1 △2 △3 △4

☐1 ☐2 ☐3

There are more ____ .

8.

△1 △2

☐1 ☐2 ☐3

There are more ____ .

Operations and Algebraic Thinking I-7

Are there more ☐ or △ ?

9.

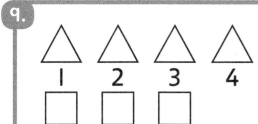

There are more ____.

10.

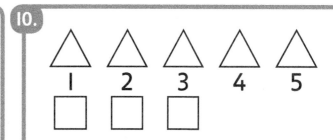

There are more ____.

11.

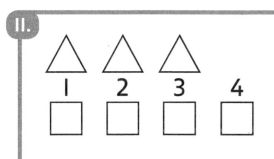

There are more ____.

12.

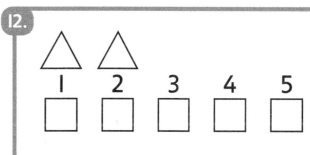

There are more ____.

13.

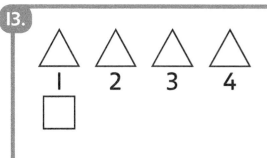

There are more ____.

14.

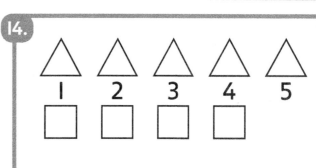

There are more ____.

15.

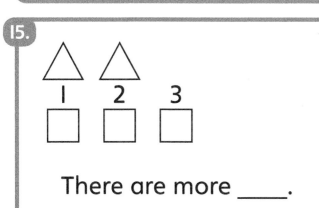

There are more ____.

16.

There are more ____.

 Are there **fewer** ☐ or △ ?

17.

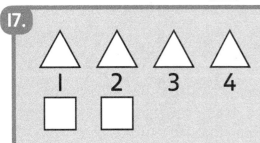

There are fewer ☐ .

18.

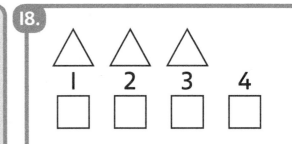

There are fewer ____ .

19.

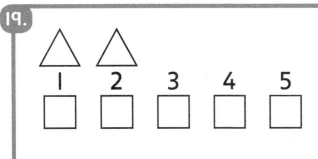

There are fewer ____ .

20.

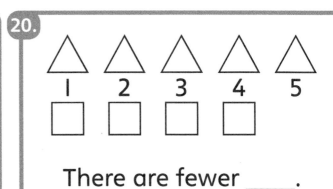

There are fewer ____ .

21.

△ △ △ △
1 2 3 4
☐

There are fewer ____ .

22.

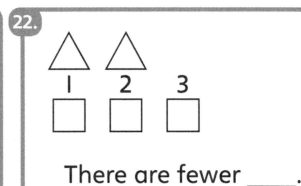

There are fewer ____ .

23.

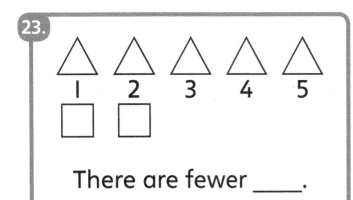

There are fewer ____ .

24.

△ △ △ △ △
1 2 3 4 5
☐ ☐ ☐

There are fewer ____ .

OAI-8 Matching

☐ Pair the ☐ and △.
☐ Are there more ☐ or △?

1.

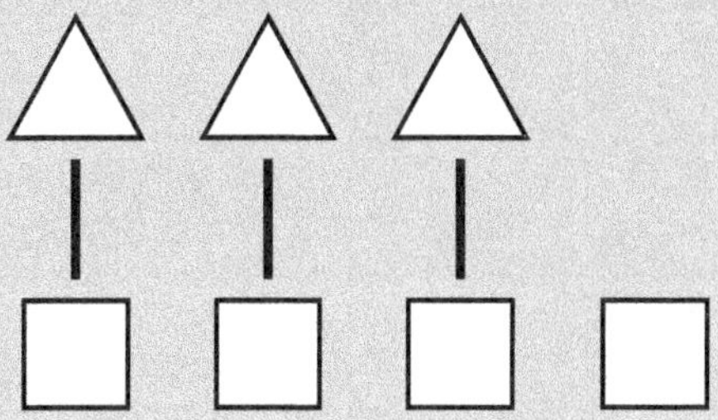

△ △ △
| | |
☐ ☐ ☐ ☐

There are more ☐.

2.

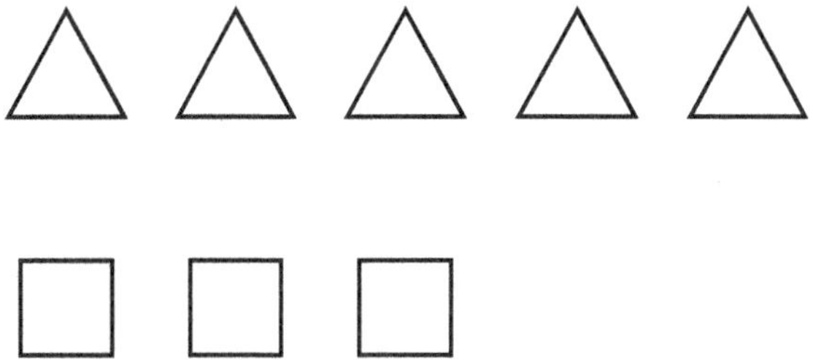

△ △ △ △ △

☐ ☐ ☐

There are more ____.

3.

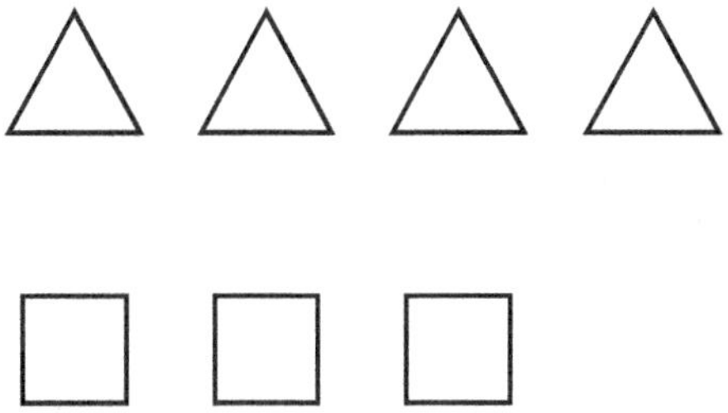

△ △ △ △

☐ ☐ ☐

There are more ____.

4.

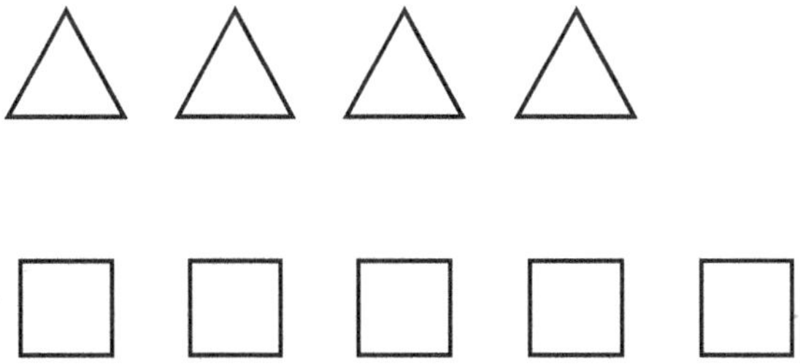

△ △ △ △

☐ ☐ ☐ ☐ ☐

There are more ____.

Can each mouse have a piece of cheese?

5.

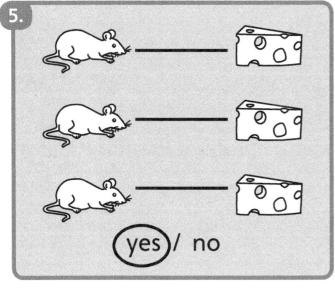

yes / no

6.

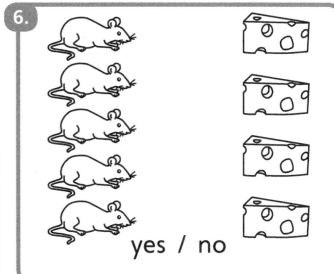

yes / no

7.

yes / no

8.

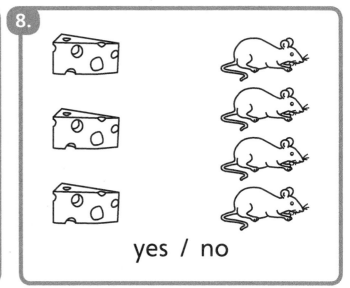

yes / no

9. BONUS

yes / no

Operations and Algebraic Thinking I-8

☐ Are there more books or people?

10.

books / (people)

11.

books / people

12. BONUS

books / people

13. BONUS

books / people

Operations and Algebraic Thinking I-8

OAI-9 How Many More?

☐ How many more ○ than △?

1.

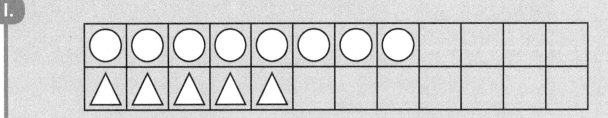

There are __3__ more ○ than △.

2.

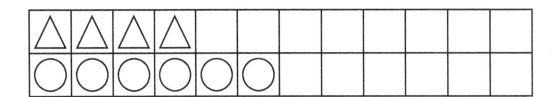

There are ____ more ○ than △.

3.

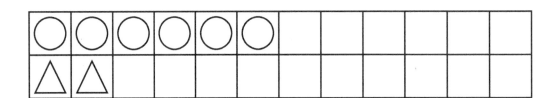

There are ____ more ○ than △.

4.

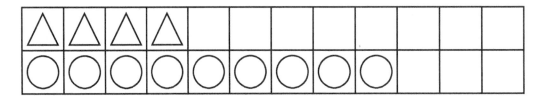

There are ____ more ○ than △.

☐ Color the extra △.
☐ How many more △ than ○?

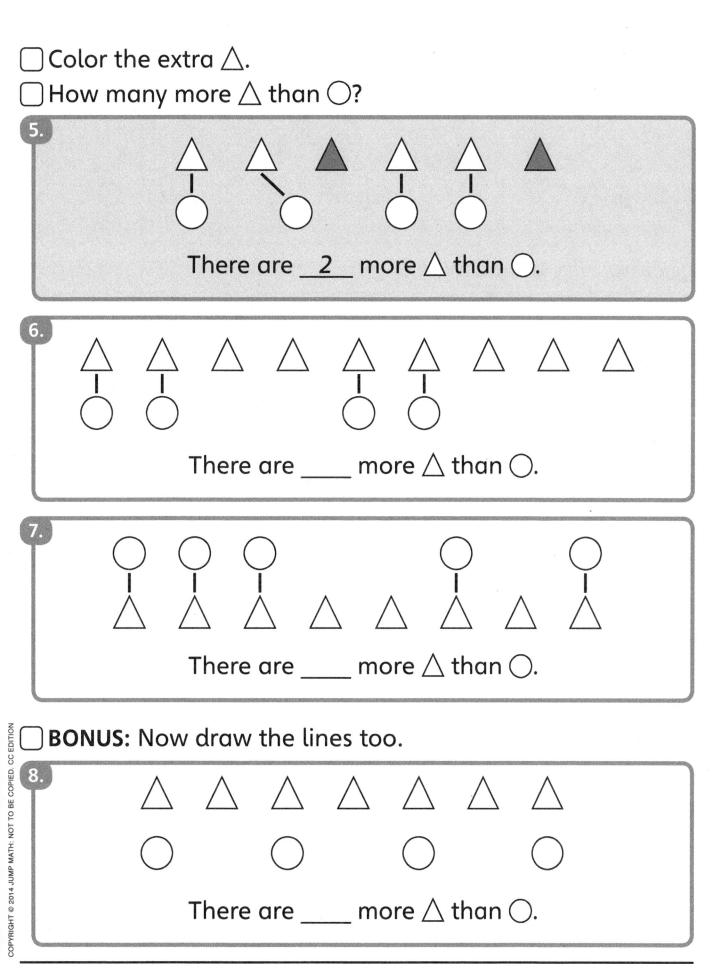

5.

There are __2__ more △ than ○.

6.

There are ____ more △ than ○.

7.

There are ____ more △ than ○.

☐ **BONUS:** Now draw the lines too.

8.

There are ____ more △ than ○.

OAI-I0 Equal

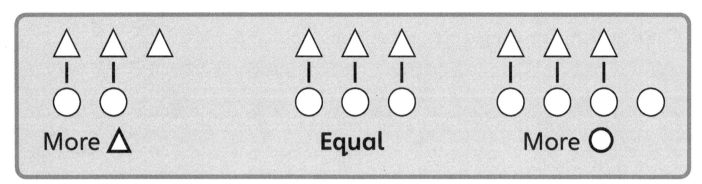

More △   Equal   More ○

☐ Write ✓ by the answer.

1.

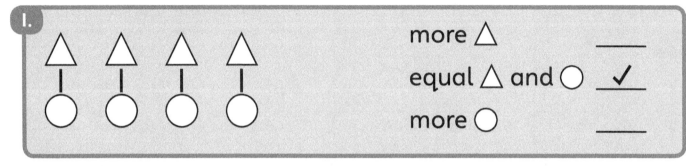

more △ _____

equal △ and ○ ✓

more ○ _____

2.

more △ _____

equal △ and ○ _____

more ○ _____

3.

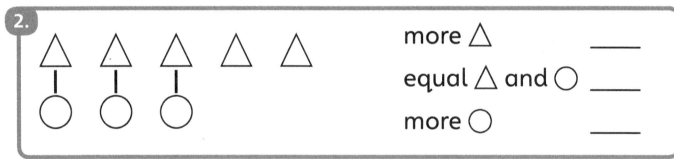

more △ _____

equal △ and ○ _____

more ○ _____

4.

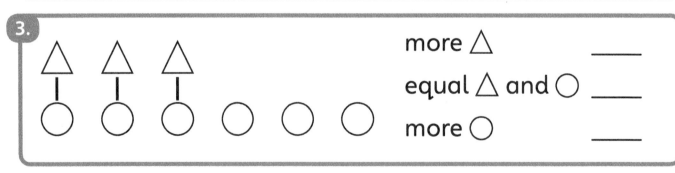

more △ _____

equal △ and ○ _____

more ○ _____

☐ Number the items.
☐ Write ✓ by the answer.

5.

1	2	3	4

① ② ③

more ☐ _____ ✓

equal ☐ and ○ _____

more ○ _____

6.

☐ ☐ ☐

○ ○ ○ ○ ○

more ☐ _____

equal ☐ and ○ _____

more ○ _____

7.

☐ ☐ ☐

○ ○ ○

more ☐ _____

equal ☐ and ○ _____

more ○ _____

8.

☐ ☐ ☐ ☐ ☐

○ ○

more ☐ _____

equal ☐ and ○ _____

more ○ _____

9.

☐ ☐ ☐ ☐

○ ○ ○ ○

more ☐ _____

equal ☐ and ○ _____

more ○ _____

OAI-11 Equal and Not Equal with Numbers

☐ Write the number of balls.
☐ Circle **equal** or **not equal**.

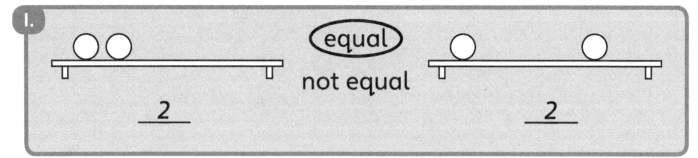

1.

equal

not equal

_2_   _2_

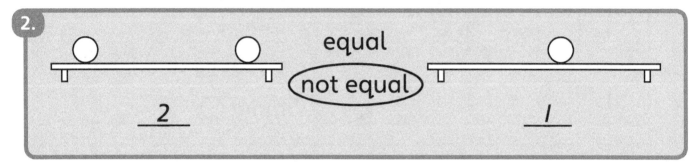

2.

equal

not equal

_2_   _1_

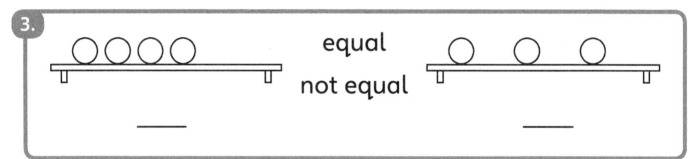

3.

equal

not equal

_____   _____

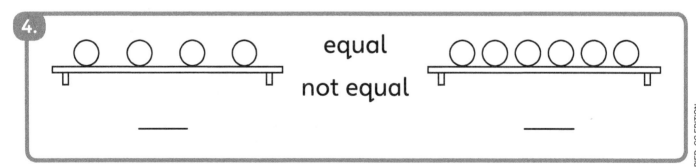

4.

equal

not equal

_____   _____

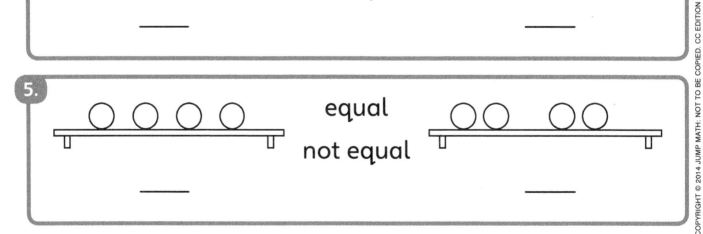

5.

equal

not equal

_____   _____

Operations and Algebraic Thinking I-II

☐ Write the number of balls.

☐ Write = if the numbers are the same.

6.

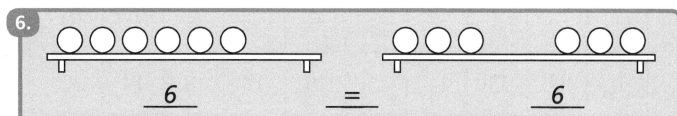

_6_   _=_   _6_

7.

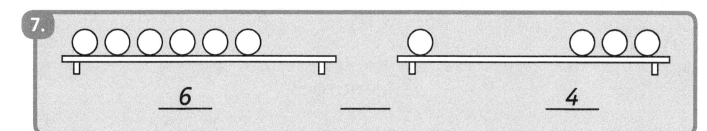

_6_   ____   _4_

8.

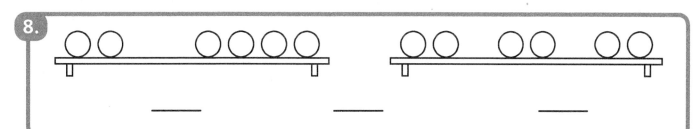

____   ____   ____

9.

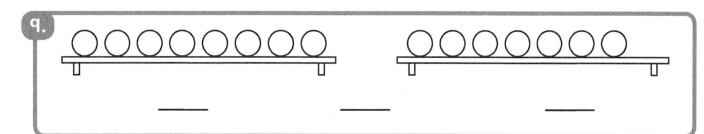

____   ____   ____

10.

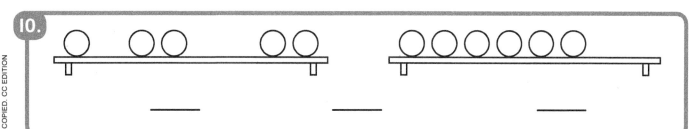

____   ____   ____

11.

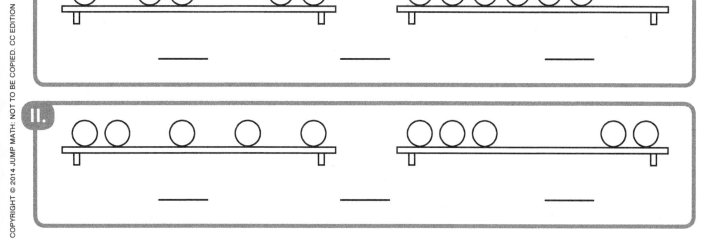

____   ____   ____

1	2	3	4	5	6	7	8	9	10
11	12	13	14	15	16	17	18	19	20

☐ Circle.

1.

13 tomatoes

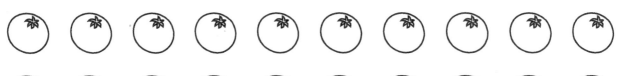

2.

12 frogs

3.

15 trees

1	2	3	4	5	6	7	8	9	10
11	12	13	14	15	16	17	18	19	20

☐ How many?

4.

___14___ stars

5.

_____ leaves

6.

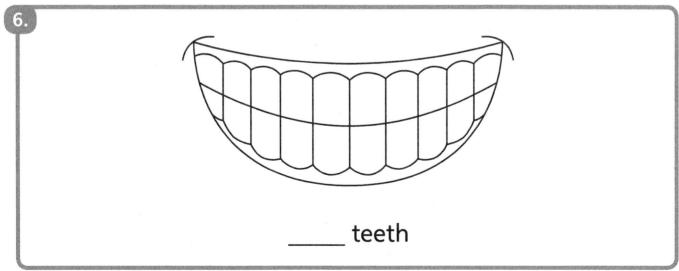

_____ teeth

NBTI-2 Using a Chart to Count to 20

☐ How many blocks?

1.

1	2	3	4	5	6	7	8	9	10
11	12	13	14	15	16	17	18	19	20

___16___ blocks

2.

1	2	3	4	5	6	7	8	9	10
11	12	13	14	15	16	17	18	19	20

_____ blocks

3.

1	2	3	4	5	6	7	8	9	10
11	12	13	14	15	16	17	18	19	20

_____ blocks

4.

1	2	3	4	5	6	7	8	9	10
11	12	13	14	15	16	17	18	19	20

_____ blocks

☐ Circle the next number in the chart.
☐ Write the number.

5.

1	2	3	④	5	6	7	8	9	10
11	12	13	14	15	16	17	18	19	20

6. 3 _4_

7. 8 _____

8. 16 _____

9.

1	2	3	4	5	6	7	8	9	10
11	12	13	14	15	16	17	18	19	20

10. 5 _____

11. 9 _____

12. 13 _____

13.

1	2	3	4	5	6	7	8	9	10
11	12	13	14	15	16	17	18	19	20

14. 17 _____

15. 2 _____

16. 11 _____

Number and Operations in Base Ten 1-2

1	2	3	4	5	6	7	8	9	10
11	12	13	14	15	16	17	18	19	20

☐ What comes next?

17. 6 _____

18. 8 _____

19. 17 _____

20. 4 _____

21. 10 _____

22. 19 _____

23. 18 _____

24. 11 _____

25. 9 _____

26. 13 _____

27. 14 _____

28. 15 _____

☐ BONUS: Cover the chart.

29. 3 _____

30. 12 _____

31. 16 _____

NBT1-3 Tens and Ones Blocks

Each circle has 10 bugs.
☐ How many bugs in all?

1.

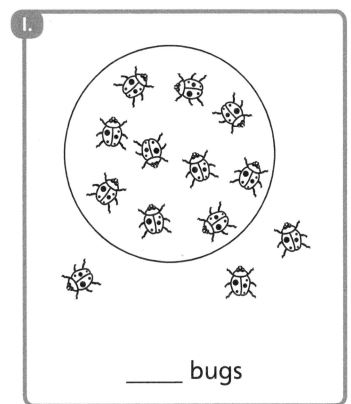

_____ bugs

2.

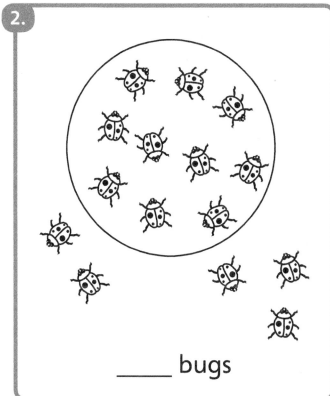

_____ bugs

3.

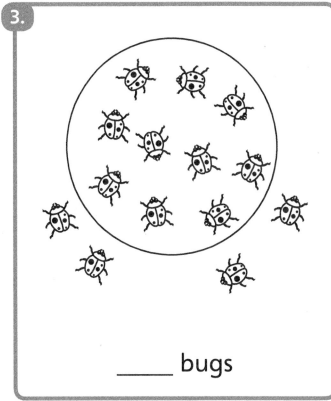

_____ bugs

4.

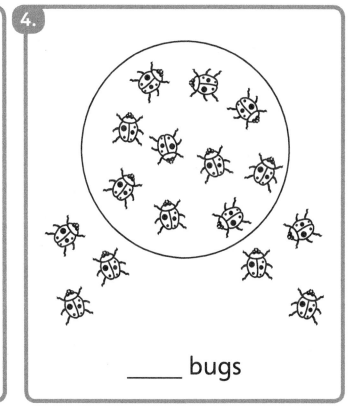

_____ bugs

Ones block   Tens block

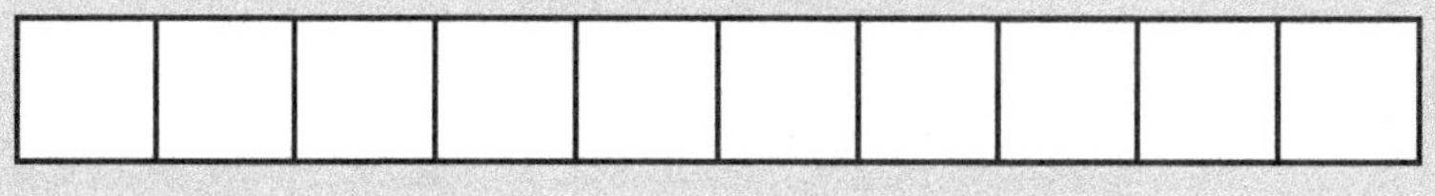

There are 10 ones blocks in a tens block.

| 1 | 2 | 3 | 4 | 5 | 6 | 7 | 8 | 9 | 10 |

| 1 | 2 | 3 | 4 | 5 | 6 | 7 | 8 | 9 | 10 |

☐ Count all the blocks.

5.

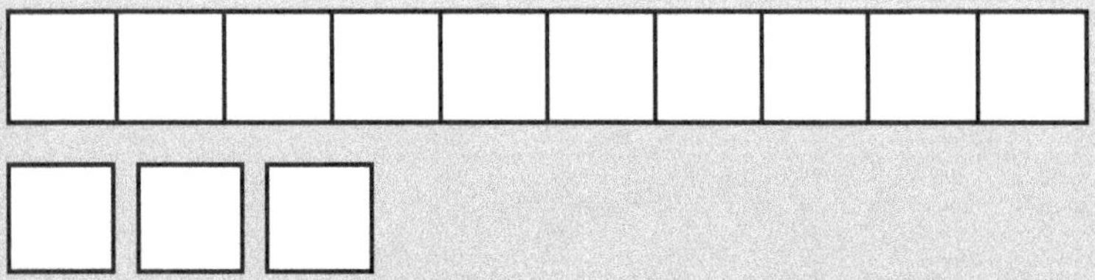

_13_ blocks in all

6.

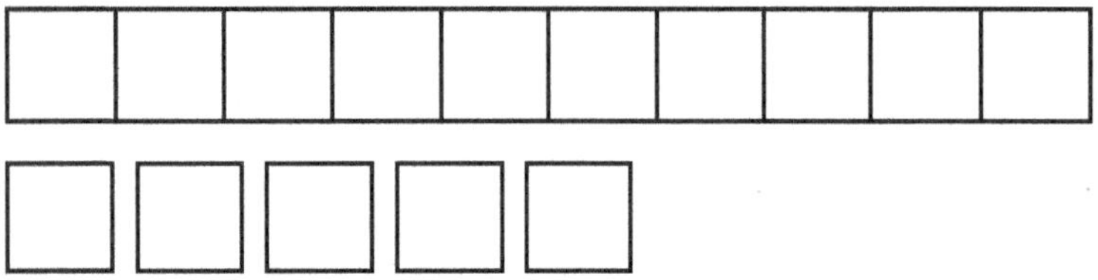

____ blocks in all

7.

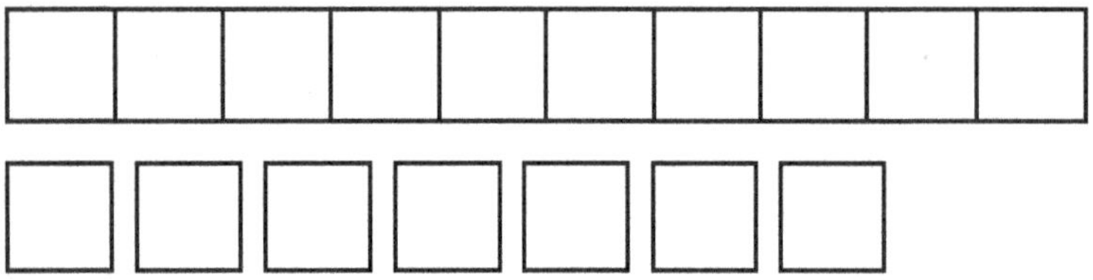

____ blocks in all

8.

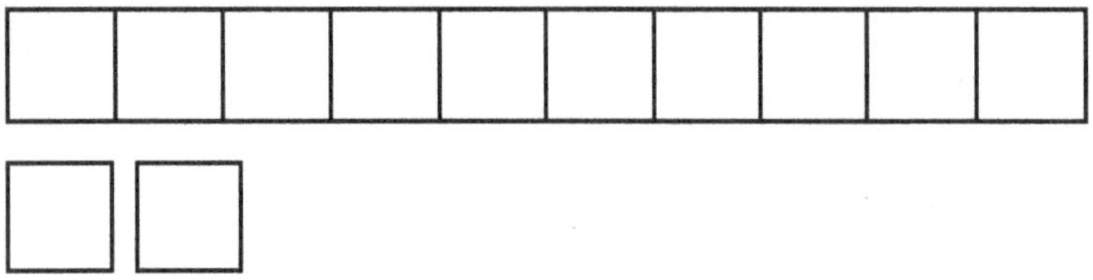

____ blocks in all

Number and Operations in Base Ten 1-3

☐ Count all the blocks.

9.

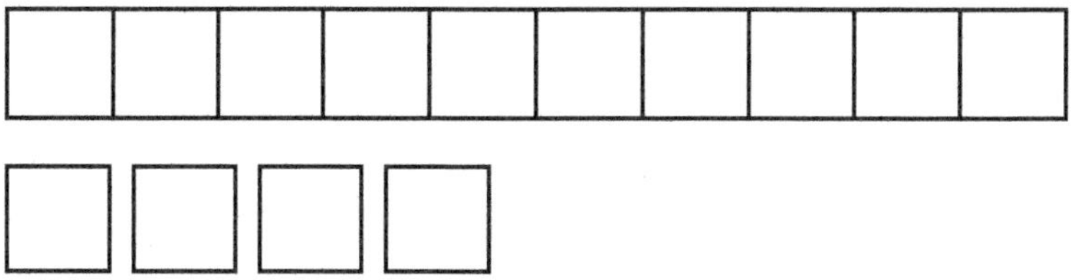

_____ blocks in all

10.

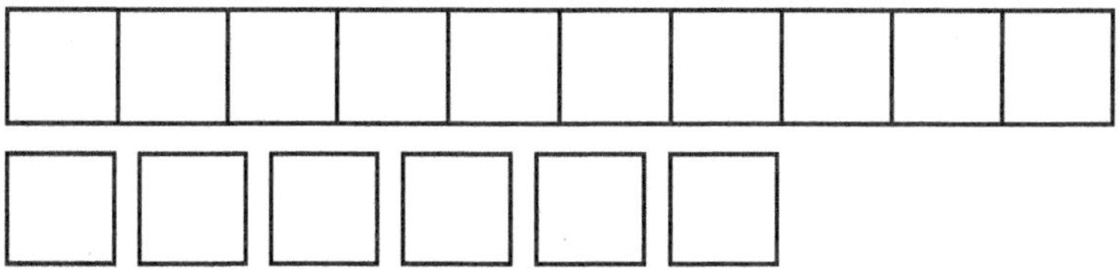

_____ blocks in all

11.

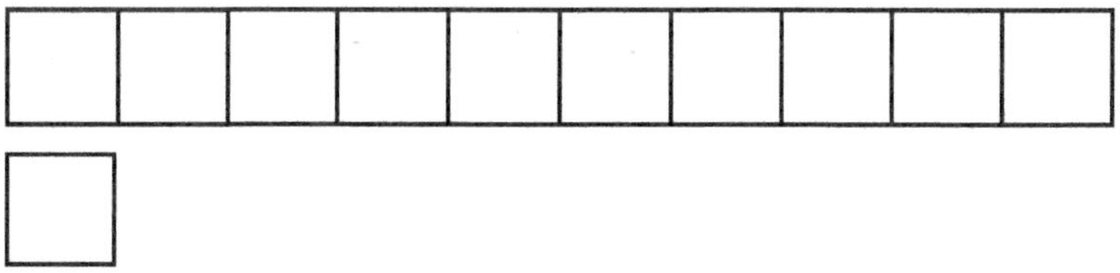

_____ blocks in all

12.

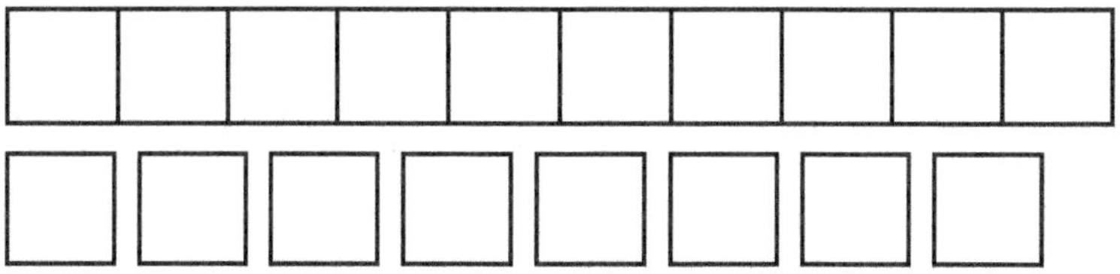

_____ blocks in all

13.

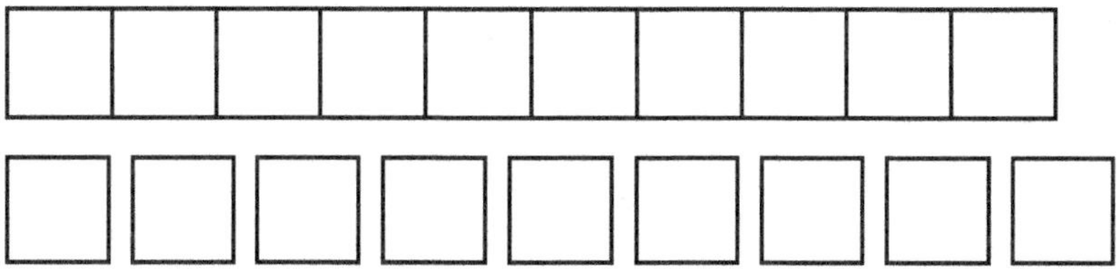

_____ blocks in all

☐ Write the numbers that come after 10 in the blocks.
☐ How many blocks in all?

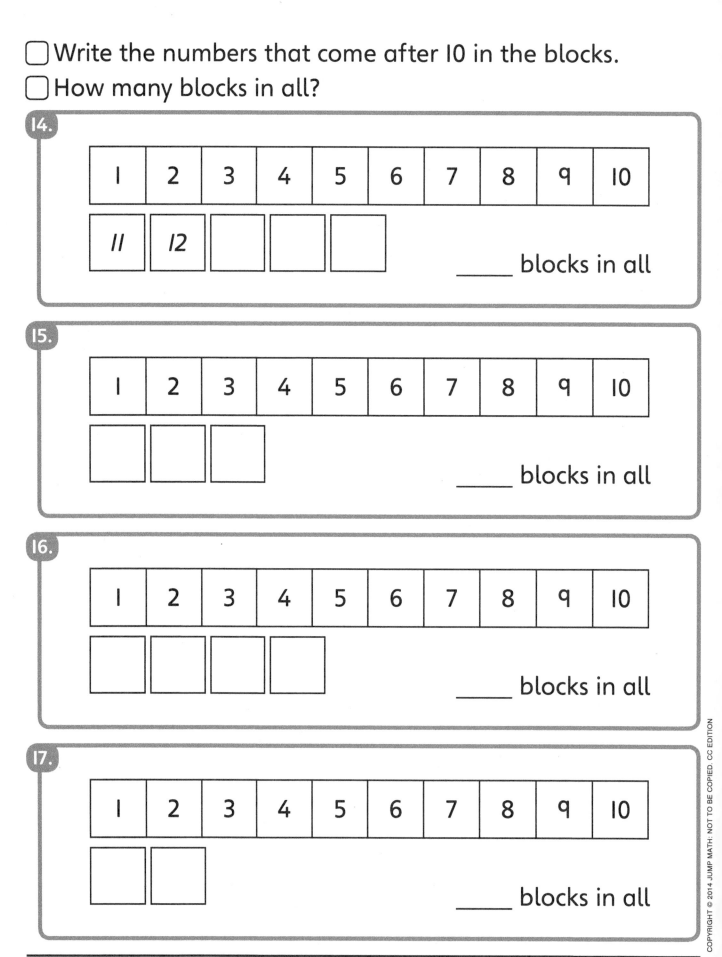

14.

| 1 | 2 | 3 | 4 | 5 | 6 | 7 | 8 | 9 | 10 |

| 11 | 12 | | | |

_____ blocks in all

15.

| 1 | 2 | 3 | 4 | 5 | 6 | 7 | 8 | 9 | 10 |

| | | |

_____ blocks in all

16.

| 1 | 2 | 3 | 4 | 5 | 6 | 7 | 8 | 9 | 10 |

| | | | |

_____ blocks in all

17.

| 1 | 2 | 3 | 4 | 5 | 6 | 7 | 8 | 9 | 10 |

| | |

_____ blocks in all

Number and Operations in Base Ten 1-3

NBT1-4 More Tens and Ones Blocks

☐ Count the **tens blocks** and **ones blocks**.

1.

1	2	3	4	5	6	7	8	9	10
11	12	13	14	15	16	17	18	19	20

18 is __1__ tens block and __8__ ones blocks.

2.

1	2	3	4	5	6	7	8	9	10
11	12	13	14	15	16	17	18	19	20

15 is _____ tens block and _____ ones blocks.

3.

1	2	3	4	5	6	7	8	9	10
11	12	13	14	15	16	17	18	19	20

17 is _____ tens block and _____ ones blocks.

4.

1	2	3	4	5	6	7	8	9	10
11	12	13	14	15	16	17	18	19	20

11 is _____ tens block and _____ ones block.

Place a tens block and a ones block on the chart.
☐ How many do you need for each number?

| 1 | 2 | 3 | 4 | 5 | 6 | 7 | 8 | 9 | 10 |
| 11 | 12 | 13 | 14 | 15 | 16 | 17 | 18 | 19 | 20 |

5.

14 is _____ tens block and _____ ones blocks.

6.

19 is _____ tens block and _____ ones blocks.

7.

16 is _____ tens block and _____ ones blocks.

8.

13 is _____ tens block and _____ ones blocks.

9.

12 is _____ tens block and _____ ones blocks.

10. BONUS

20 is __*1*__ tens block and _____ ones blocks.

Hundreds chart:

1	2	3	4	5	6	7	8	9	10
11	12	13	14	15	16	17	18	19	20

Tens and ones blocks:

14 is 1 ten and 4 ones.

What number do the blocks show?

11.

1 ten and 6 ones is __16__.

12.

1 ten and 1 one is _____.

13.

1 ten and 5 ones is _____.

14.

1 ten and 3 ones is _____.

15.

1 ten and 9 ones is _____.

16.

1 ten and 7 ones is _____.

NBTI-5 Greater Than with Charts

6 is 6 ones. | 1 | 2 | 3 | 4 | 5 | 6 | 7 | 8 | 9 | 10 |

4 is 4 ones. | 1 | 2 | 3 | 4 | 5 | 6 | 7 | 8 | 9 | 10 |

6 is **greater than** 4.

☐ Circle the greater number.

1.

| 1 | 2 | 3 | 4 | 5 | 6 | 7 | 8 | 9 | 10 |

| 1 | 2 | 3 | 4 | 5 | 6 | 7 | 8 | 9 | 10 |

⑦
3

2.

| 1 | 2 | 3 | 4 | 5 | 6 | 7 | 8 | 9 | 10 |

| 1 | 2 | 3 | 4 | 5 | 6 | 7 | 8 | 9 | 10 |

3
5

3.

| 1 | 2 | 3 | 4 | 5 | 6 | 7 | 8 | 9 | 10 |

| 1 | 2 | 3 | 4 | 5 | 6 | 7 | 8 | 9 | 10 |

4
6

4.

| 1 | 2 | 3 | 4 | 5 | 6 | 7 | 8 | 9 | 10 |

| 1 | 2 | 3 | 4 | 5 | 6 | 7 | 8 | 9 | 10 |

9
1

Number and Operations in Base Ten I-5

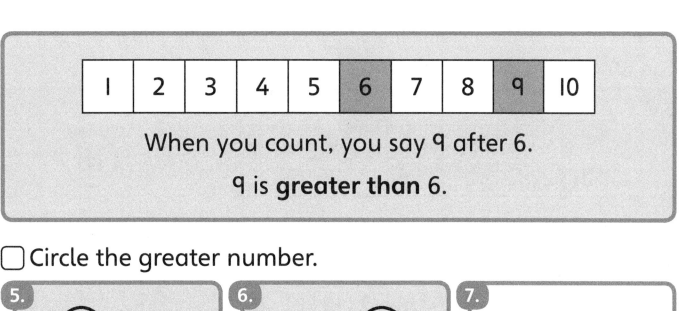

When you count, you say 9 after 6.

9 is **greater than** 6.

☐ Circle the greater number.

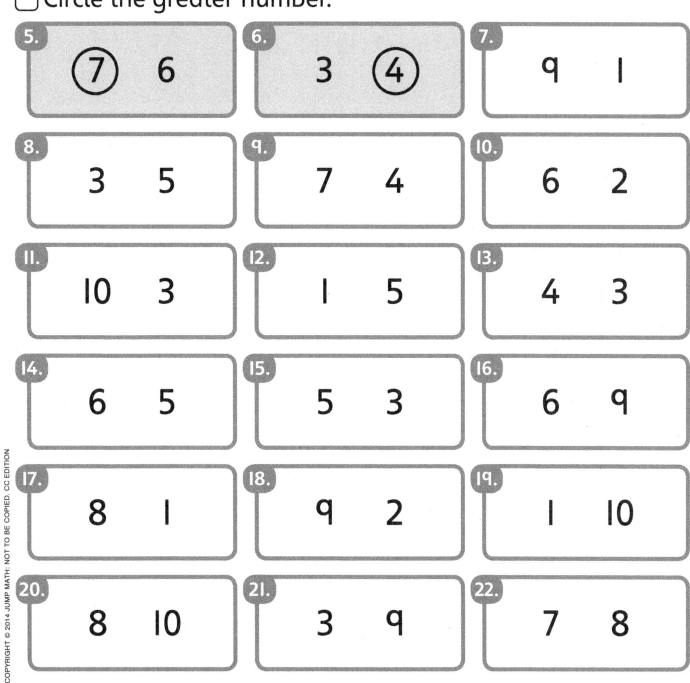

5. (7) 6

6. 3 (4)

7. 9 1

8. 3 5

9. 7 4

10. 6 2

11. 10 3

12. 1 5

13. 4 3

14. 6 5

15. 5 3

16. 6 9

17. 8 1

18. 9 2

19. 1 10

20. 8 10

21. 3 9

22. 7 8

NBTI-6 Greater Than with Charts (Tens and Ones)

☐ Circle the greater number.

1.

1	2	3	4	5	6	7	8	9	10
11	12	13	14	15	16	17	18	19	20

(16)

1	2	3	4	5	6	7	8	9	10
11	12	13	14	15	16	17	18	19	20

14

2.

1	2	3	4	5	6	7	8	9	10
11	12	13	14	15	16	17	18	19	20

17

1	2	3	4	5	6	7	8	9	10
11	12	13	14	15	16	17	18	19	20

12

3.

1	2	3	4	5	6	7	8	9	10
11	12	13	14	15	16	17	18	19	20

11

1	2	3	4	5	6	7	8	9	10
11	12	13	14	15	16	17	18	19	20

15

1	2	3	4	5	6	7	8	9	10
11	12	13	14	15	16	17	18	19	20

When you count, you say 15 after 12.

15 is greater than 12.

☐ Circle the greater number.

4. 12   (14)

5. 11   15

6. 20   15

7. 13   19

8. 14   17

9. 8   9

10. 11   9

11. 12   10

12. 15   8

13. 20   16

14. 13   14

15. 14   19

16. 1   19

17. 2   18

18. 3   7

19. 6   12

20. 7   13

21. 16   4

1	2	3	4	5	6	7	8	9	10
11	12	13	14	15	16	17	18	19	20

☐ Circle the numbers that are greater than 10.

22.

5 12 7 13 2 18

☐ Circle the greater number.

23.
10 2

24.
3 10

25.
10 17

26.
5 10

27.
16 10

28.
13 10

☐ Circle the greater number.

29.
5 11

30.
17 4

31.
3 12

32.
8 16

33.
13 5

34.
19 1

Number and Operations in Base Ten 1-6

NBTI-7 Greater Than

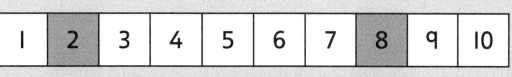

| 1 | 2 | 3 | 4 | 5 | 6 | 7 | 8 | 9 | 10 |

When you count, you say 8 after 2.

8 is **greater than** 2.

☐ Circle **Yes** or **No**.

1.

9 is greater than 1.

(Yes)   No

2.

8 is greater than 2.

Yes   No

3.

3 is greater than 9.

Yes   No

4.

10 is greater than 5.

Yes   No

5.

8 is greater than 10.

Yes   No

6.

7 is greater than 13.

Yes   No

7.

14 is greater than 2.

Yes   No

8.

17 is greater than 16.

Yes   No

Circle the greater number.
Put the numbers in the correct places.

9.

6   (8)

__8__ is greater than __6__.

10.

(10)   7

__10__ is greater than __7__.

11.

5   2

_____ is greater than _____.

12.

3   9

_____ is greater than _____.

13.

7   6

_____ is greater than _____.

14.

8   6

_____ is greater than _____.

15.

13   18

_____ is greater than _____.

16.

9   12

_____ is greater than _____.

17.

20   15

_____ is greater than _____.

18.

1   11

_____ is greater than _____.

19.

12   7

_____ is greater than _____.

20.

17   20

_____ is greater than _____.

NBTI-8 Less Than

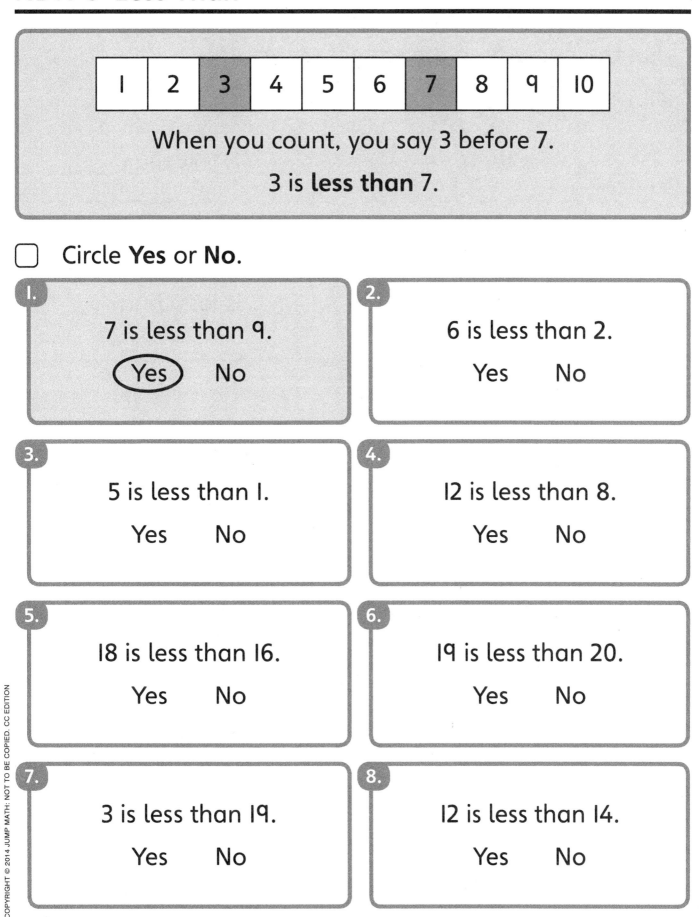

| 1 | 2 | **3** | 4 | 5 | 6 | **7** | 8 | 9 | 10 |

When you count, you say 3 before 7.

3 is **less than** 7.

☐ Circle **Yes** or **No**.

1.
7 is less than 9.

(Yes)   No

2.
6 is less than 2.

Yes   No

3.
5 is less than 1.

Yes   No

4.
12 is less than 8.

Yes   No

5.
18 is less than 16.

Yes   No

6.
19 is less than 20.

Yes   No

7.
3 is less than 19.

Yes   No

8.
12 is less than 14.

Yes   No

☐ Circle the number that is less.
☐ Put the numbers in the correct places.

9.

9　　⑤

__5__ is less than __9__.

10.

6　　4

____ is less than ____.

11.

4　　8

____ is less than ____.

12.

2　　9

____ is less than ____.

13.

7　　2

____ is less than ____.

14.

13　　11

____ is less than ____.

15.

16　　19

____ is less than ____.

16.

20　　5

____ is less than ____.

17.

18　　11

____ is less than ____.

18.

12　　14

____ is less than ____.

19.

16　　14

____ is less than ____.

20.

3　　17

____ is less than ____.

Number and Operations in Base Ten 1-8

☐ Circle the correct answer.

1.

7   is greater than   9

(is less than)

2.

8   (is greater than)   2

is less than

3.

12   is greater than   3

is less than

4.

4   is greater than   9

is less than

5.

13   is greater than   19

is less than

6.

20   is greater than   15

is less than

7.

11   is greater than   2

is less than

8.

17   is greater than   6

is less than

9.

18   is greater than   17

is less than

10.

16   is greater than   1

is less than

11.

5   is greater than   8

is less than

12.

14   is greater than   13

is less than

Circle **Yes** or **No**.

13.
9 is greater than 3.

Yes No

14.
10 is less than 4.

Yes No

15.
3 is less than 7.

Yes No

16.
5 is less than 2.

Yes No

17.
12 is greater than 6.

Yes No

18.
19 is less than 20.

Yes No

19.
7 is greater than 14.

Yes No

20.
16 is greater than 18.

Yes No

21.
19 is greater than 17.

Yes No

22.
20 is less than 5.

Yes No

23.
12 is greater than 9.

Yes No

24.
16 is less than 4.

Yes No

⬜ Circle the greater number.
⬜ Put the numbers in the correct places.

25.

8   (16)

_16_ is greater than _8_ .

_8_ is less than _16_ .

26.

15   12

____ is greater than ____ .

____ is less than ____ .

27.

3   11

____ is greater than ____ .

____ is less than ____ .

28.

14   19

____ is greater than ____ .

____ is less than ____ .

29.

2   18

____ is greater than ____ .

____ is less than ____ .

30.

1   3

____ is greater than ____ .

____ is less than ____ .

31. BONUS

8   6

____ is less than ____ .

____ is greater than ____ .

32. BONUS

17   9

____ is less than ____ .

____ is greater than ____ .

☐ Put the numbers in the correct places.

33.

7   2

_____ is greater than _____.

34.

5   10

_____ is less than _____.

35.

8   1

_____ is greater than _____.

36.

9   15

_____ is greater than _____.

37.

20   12

_____ is greater than _____.

38.

16   19

_____ is less than _____.

39.

11   5

_____ is less than _____.

40.

2   13

_____ is greater than _____.

41.

17   8

_____ is less than _____.

42.

13   6

_____ is less than _____.

43.

19   14

_____ is greater than _____.

44.

15   18

_____ is less than _____.

NBTI-I0 Ordering Numbers Up to 20

☐ Write the ▢ numbers from **smallest** to **largest**.

I.

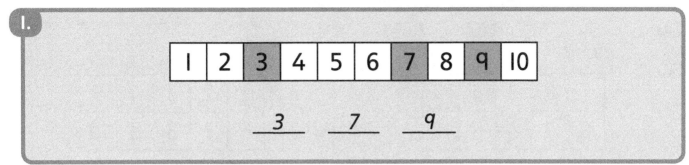

| 1 | 2 | 3 | 4 | 5 | 6 | 7 | 8 | 9 | 10 |

___3___   ___7___   ___9___

2.

| 1 | 2 | 3 | 4 | 5 | 6 | 7 | 8 | 9 | 10 |

_____   _____   _____

3.

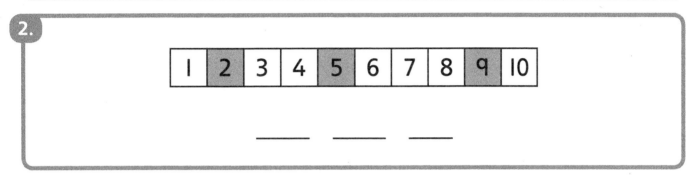

| 1 | 2 | 3 | 4 | 5 | 6 | 7 | 8 | 9 | 10 |
| 11 | 12 | 13 | 14 | 15 | 16 | 17 | 18 | 19 | 20 |

____ ____ ____ ____ ____ ____ ____ ____

4.

1	2	3	4	5
6	7	8	9	10
11	12	13	14	15
16	17	18	19	20

____ ____ ____

5.

1	2	3	4	5
6	7	8	9	10
11	12	13	14	15
16	17	18	19	20

____ ____ ____

Shade the given numbers.

Order them from smallest to largest.

6.

5 8 2

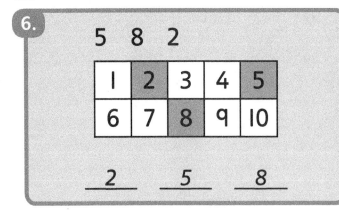

1	2	3	4	5
6	7	8	9	10

_2_ _5_ _8_

7.

10 6 1

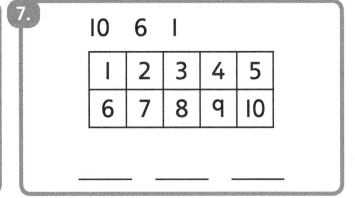

1	2	3	4	5
6	7	8	9	10

___ ___ ___

8.

16 13 14

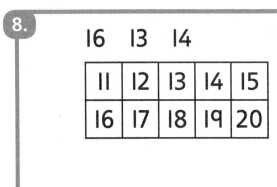

11	12	13	14	15
16	17	18	19	20

___ ___ ___

9.

11 20 17

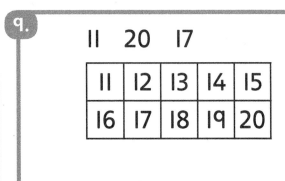

11	12	13	14	15
16	17	18	19	20

___ ___ ___

10.

14 6 3 19 10

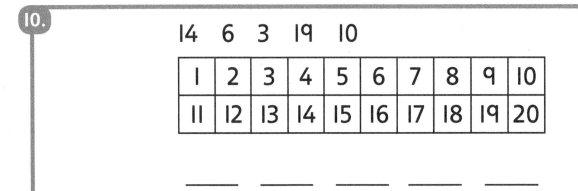

1	2	3	4	5	6	7	8	9	10
11	12	13	14	15	16	17	18	19	20

___ ___ ___ ___ ___

11.

2 17 4 8 16

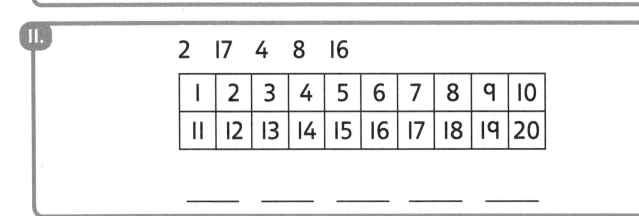

1	2	3	4	5	6	7	8	9	10
11	12	13	14	15	16	17	18	19	20

___ ___ ___ ___ ___

Number and Operations in Base Ten 1-10

OAI-I2 Adding

 Add by counting.

1.

4   +   3   =   _____

2.

3   +   5   =   _____

3.

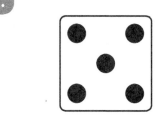

5   +   2   =   _____

4.

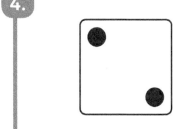   

2   +   6   =   _____

☐ Draw circles to add.

5.

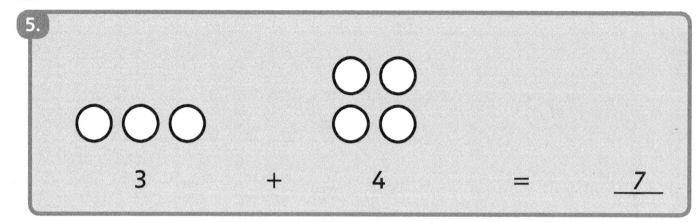

3   +   4   =   _7_

6.

2   +   3   =   ____

7.

1   +   4   =   ____

8.

3   +   3   =   ____

Operations and Algebraic Thinking 1-12

☐ How many in total?

9.

3 flags   +   2 flags   =   _____ flags in total

3 balls   +   2 balls   =   _____ balls in total

3 + 2 = _____

10.

_____ trees in total   =   2 trees   +   4 trees

_____ children   =   2 girls   +   4 boys

_____ = 2 + 4

OAI-13 More Adding

☐ Add.

1.
☆☆
☆

$$\begin{array}{r} 2 \\ + 1 \\ \hline \end{array}$$

2.
☆☆
☆☆☆

$$\begin{array}{r} 2 \\ + 3 \\ \hline \end{array}$$

3.
☆
☆☆☆
☆☆
☆☆☆

$$\begin{array}{r} 1 \\ 3 \\ 2 \\ + 3 \\ \hline \end{array}$$

4.
☆☆
☆☆

$$\begin{array}{r} 2 \\ + 2 \\ \hline \end{array}$$

5.
☆
☆☆☆☆

$$\begin{array}{r} 1 \\ + 4 \\ \hline \end{array}$$

☐ How many crayons in all?

6.
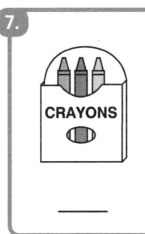

$$\underline{\quad 2 \quad}$$

7.

$$\underline{\qquad}$$

8.
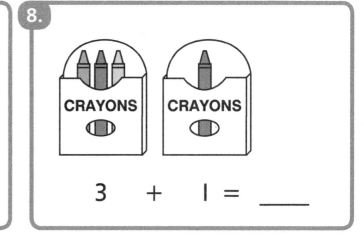

$$3 \ + \ 1 \ = \ \underline{\qquad}$$

9.
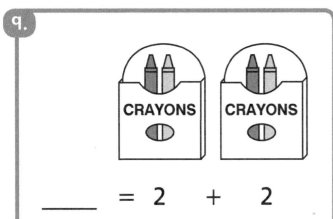

$$\underline{\qquad} \ = \ 2 \ + \ 2$$

10.
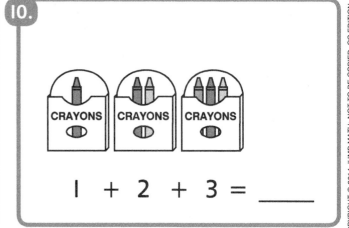

$$1 \ + \ 2 \ + \ 3 \ = \ \underline{\qquad}$$

☐ Draw a picture to add.

11.

3   +   2   +   6   =   __11__

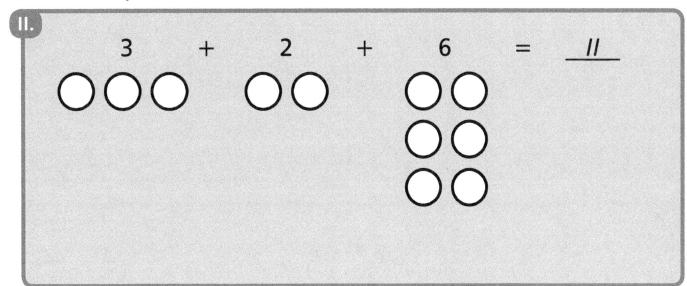

12.

4   +   2   +   3   =   ____

13.

```
  3
  2
+ 5
____
```

14.

```
  4
  2
+ 7
____
```

Operations and Algebraic Thinking 1-13

☐ Add 0.

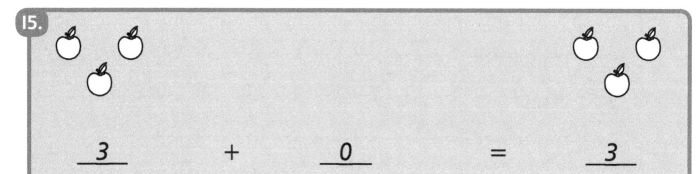

15.

$$\underline{3} \quad + \quad \underline{0} \quad = \quad \underline{3}$$

16.

$$\underline{} \quad + \quad \underline{} \quad = \quad \underline{}$$

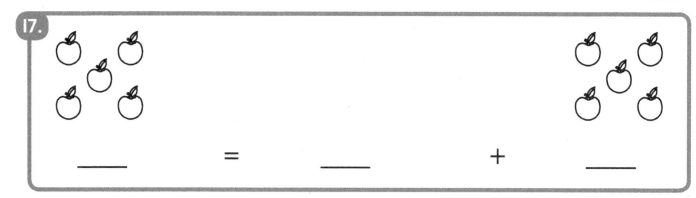

17.

$$\underline{} \quad = \quad \underline{} \quad + \quad \underline{}$$

18.

$$\underline{} \quad = \quad \underline{} \quad + \quad \underline{}$$

19. BONUS

$$0 + 17 = \underline{}$$

20. BONUS

$$\underline{} = 14 + 0$$

Operations and Algebraic Thinking 1-13

OAI-14 Addition and Order

 Add.

1.

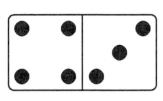

$\underline{4} + \underline{3} = \underline{7}$

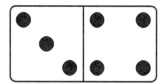

$\underline{} + \underline{} = \underline{}$

2.

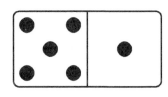

$\underline{} + \underline{} = \underline{}$

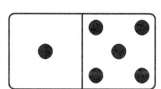

$\underline{} + \underline{} = \underline{}$

3.

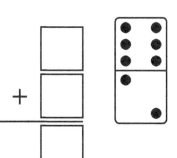

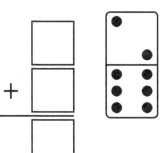

4.

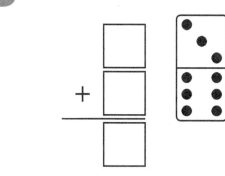

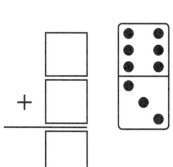

☐ Write one addition sentence for both pictures.

5.

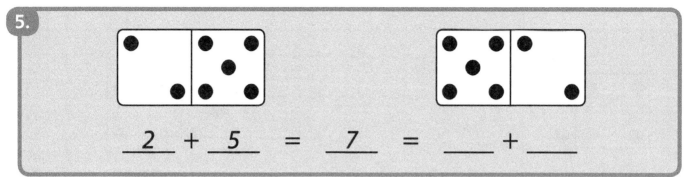

$\underline{\ 2\ } + \underline{\ 5\ } = \underline{\ 7\ } = \underline{\ \ \ \ } + \underline{\ \ \ \ }$

6.

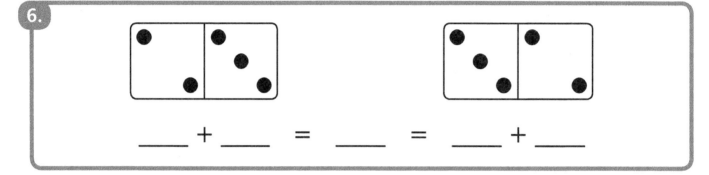

$\underline{\ \ \ \ } + \underline{\ \ \ \ } = \underline{\ \ \ \ } = \underline{\ \ \ \ } + \underline{\ \ \ \ }$

7.

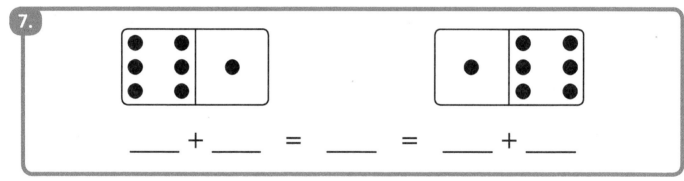

$\underline{\ \ \ \ } + \underline{\ \ \ \ } = \underline{\ \ \ \ } = \underline{\ \ \ \ } + \underline{\ \ \ \ }$

8. **9.**

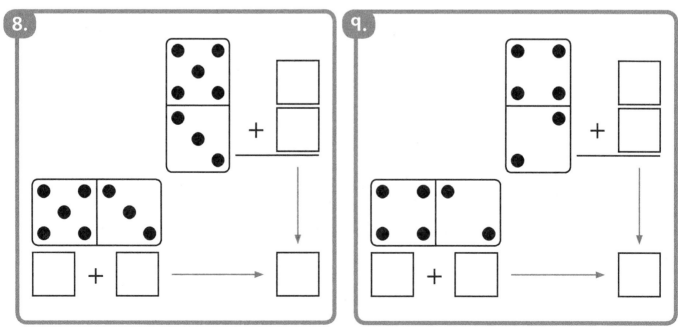

Operations and Algebraic Thinking 1-14

OAI-15 Adding Using a Chart

☐ Add.

1.

| 1 | 2 | 3 | ④ | ⑤ | ⑥ | ⑦ | 8 | 9 | 10 |

3 + 4 = _____

2.

| 1 | 2 | ③ | ④ | ⑤ | ⑥ | ⑦ | ⑧ | ⑨ | 10 |

2 + 7 = _____

3.

| 1 | 2 | 3 | 4 | 5 | 6 | ⑦ | ⑧ | 9 | 10 |

6 + 2 = _____

4.

| 1 | 2 | 3 | 4 | 5 | 6 | 7 | 8 | 9 | ⑩ |
| ⑪ | ⑫ | 13 | 14 | 15 | 16 | 17 | 18 | 19 | 20 |

9 + 3 = _____

5.

| 1 | 2 | 3 | 4 | 5 | 6 | 7 | 8 | ⑨ | ⑩ |
| ⑪ | ⑫ | ⑬ | 14 | 15 | 16 | 17 | 18 | 19 | 20 |

8 + 5 = _____

☐ Shade the first number of squares.
☐ Circle the second number of squares.
☐ Add.

6.

1	2	3	④	⑤	⑥	⑦	⑧	9	10

$3 + 5 = \underline{\ 8\ }$

7.

1	2	3	4	5	6	7	8	9	10

$4 + 5 = \underline{\quad}$

8.

1	2	3	4	5	6	7	8	9	10

$8 + 1 = \underline{\quad}$

9.

1	2	3	4	5	6	7	8	9	10

$7 + 3 = \underline{\quad}$

10.

1	2	3	4	5	6	7	8	9	10
11	12	13	14	15	16	17	18	19	20

$12 + 6 = \underline{\quad}$

Operations and Algebraic Thinking 1-15

The square showing the first number is shaded.
☐ Add 3 by circling the next 3 numbers.

11.

| 1 | 2 | 3 | 4 | 5 | ⑥ | ⑦ | ⑧ | 9 | 10 |

$5 + 3 = \underline{\ 8\ }$

12.

| 1 | 2 | 3 | 4 | 5 | 6 | 7 | 8 | 9 | 10 |
| 11 | 12 | 13 | 14 | 15 | 16 | 17 | 18 | 19 | 20 |

$9 + 3 = \underline{\qquad}$

13.

| 1 | 2 | 3 | 4 | 5 | 6 | 7 | 8 | 9 | 10 |
| 11 | 12 | 13 | 14 | 15 | 16 | 17 | 18 | 19 | 20 |

$7 + 3 = \underline{\qquad}$

14.

1	2	3	4	5
6	7	8	9	10
11	12	13	14	15
16	17	18	19	20

$13 + 3 = \underline{\qquad}$

15.

1	2	3	4	5
6	7	8	9	10
11	12	13	14	15
16	17	18	19	20

$15 + 3 = \underline{\qquad}$

☐ Shade the square showing the first number.
☐ Circle the second number of squares.
☐ Add.

16.

1	2	3	4	5	⑥	⑦	8	9	10

$$5 + 2 = \underline{\quad 7 \quad}$$

17.

1	2	3	4	5	6	7	8	9	10

$$6 + 3 = \underline{\qquad}$$

18.

1	2	3	4	5	6	7	8	9	10
11	12	13	14	15	16	17	18	19	20

$$8 + 5 = \underline{\qquad}$$

19.

1	2	3	4	5
6	7	8	9	10
11	12	13	14	15

$$4 + 7 = \underline{\qquad}$$

20.

1	2	3	4	5
6	7	8	9	10
11	12	13	14	15

$$9 + 5 = \underline{\qquad}$$

Operations and Algebraic Thinking 1-15

OAI-16 Counting On to Add 1 or 2

☐ Shade the **next** circle.
☐ Add 1.

1.
1 2 3 4

3 + 1 = __4__

2.
1 2 3 4 5

4 + 1 = ____

3.
1 2 3

2 + 1 = ____

4.
1 2 3 4 5 6

5 + 1 = ____

5.
1 2 3 4 5 6 7 8 9 10

7 + 1 = ____

6.
1 2 3 4 5 6 7 8 9 10

8 + 1 = ____

☐ Find the **next** number.

☐ Add I.

7.

1 2 3 4 5

4 + 1 = _5_

8.

1 2 **3** 4 5

3 + 1 = ____

9.

1 2 3 4 **5** 6 7

5 + 1 = ____

10.

1 2 3 4 5 **6** 7

6 + 1 = ____

11.

1 2 3 4 5 6 7 8 9 10

7 + 1 = ____

12.

1 2 3 4 5 6 7 8 9 10

9 + 1 = ____

13.

2 + 1 = ____

14.

8 + 1 = ____

15. BONUS

14 + 1 = ____

☐ Find the **next 2** numbers.

☐ Add 2.

16.

1 2 3 **4** 5 6 7

$4 + 2 = \underline{6}$

17.

1 2 **3** 4 5 6 7

$3 + 2 = \underline{}$

18.

1 2 3 4 5 **6** 7 8

$6 + 2 = \underline{}$

19.

1 2 3 4 **5** 6 7 8

$5 + 2 = \underline{}$

20.

1 2 3 4 5 6 7 8 9 10 11 12

$8 + 2 = \underline{}$

21.

1 2 3 4 5 6 7 8 9 10 11 12

$9 + 2 = \underline{}$

22.

$2 + 2 = \underline{}$

23.

$10 + 2 = \underline{}$

24. BONUS

$17 + 2 = \underline{}$

Operations and Algebraic Thinking 1-16

☐ Add by counting on.

I.

5   _6_   _7_   5 + 2 = _7_

2.

4   ___   ___   ___   4 + 3 = ___

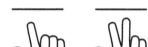

3.

6   ___   ___   ___   6 + 4 = ___

4.

7   ___   ___   ___   7 + 4 = ___

5.

8   ___   ___   8 + 2 = ___

6.

5 + 3 = ___

7.

3 + 5 = ___

8.

7 + 3 = ___

There are **5** apples in the bag.

☐ Add by counting on.

9.

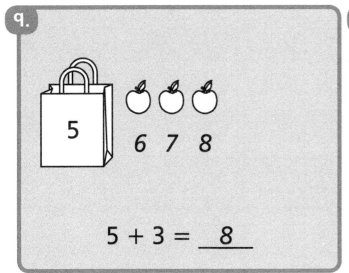

6 7 8

5 + 3 = __8__

10.

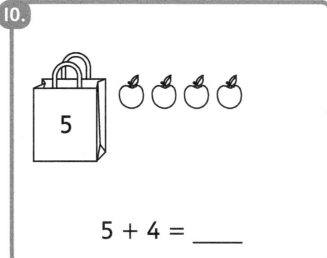

5 + 4 = ____

11.

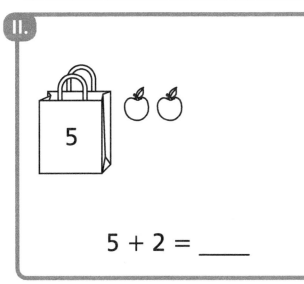

5 + 2 = ____

12.

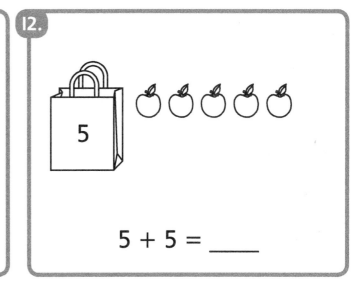

5 + 5 = ____

13.

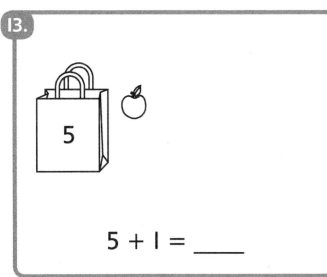

5 + 1 = ____

14.

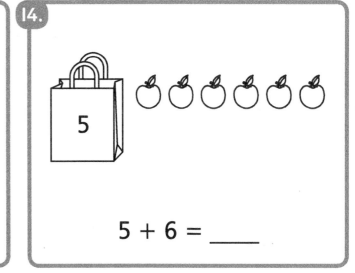

5 + 6 = ____

☐ Add by counting on from each number.

1.

$$7 + 3 = \underline{10}$$

7 $\underline{8}$ $\underline{9}$ $\underline{10}$

3 $\underline{4}$ $\underline{5}$ $\underline{6}$ $\underline{7}$ $\underline{8}$ $\underline{9}$ $\underline{10}$

2.

$$4 + 8 = \underline{}$$

4 $\underline{}$ $\underline{}$ $\underline{}$ $\underline{}$ $\underline{}$ $\underline{}$ $\underline{}$ $\underline{}$

8 $\underline{}$ $\underline{}$ $\underline{}$ $\underline{}$

3.

$$9 + 2 = \underline{}$$

9 $\underline{}$ $\underline{}$

2 $\underline{}$ $\underline{}$ $\underline{}$ $\underline{}$ $\underline{}$ $\underline{}$ $\underline{}$ $\underline{}$ $\underline{}$

4.

$$3 + 10 = \underline{}$$

3 $\underline{}$ $\underline{}$ $\underline{}$ $\underline{}$ $\underline{}$ $\underline{}$ $\underline{}$ $\underline{}$ $\underline{}$ $\underline{}$

10 $\underline{}$ $\underline{}$ $\underline{}$

☐ Trace the correct number of blanks.

☐ Add by counting on from each number.

5.

$$2 + 5 = \underline{\ 7\ }$$

2   _3_   _4_   _5_   _6_   _7_   ----- ----- -----

5   _6_   _7_   ----- ----- ----- ----- -----

6.

$$7 + 4 = \underline{\qquad}$$

7   ----- ----- ----- ----- ----- ----- -----

4   ----- ----- ----- ----- ----- ----- -----

7.

$$3 + 6 = \underline{\qquad}$$

3   ----- ----- ----- ----- ----- -----

6   ----- ----- ----- ----- ----- -----

☐ Circle the correct word.

8.

Counting on from the   bigger / smaller   number is easier

because there are   more / fewer   numbers to count.

OAI-19 Using Number Lines to Add

The frog takes 2 jumps.
◯ Where does it end up?

1.

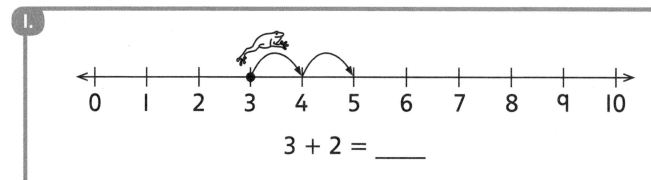

$$3 + 2 = \underline{}$$

2.

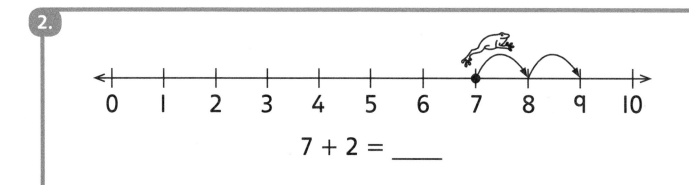

$$7 + 2 = \underline{}$$

3.

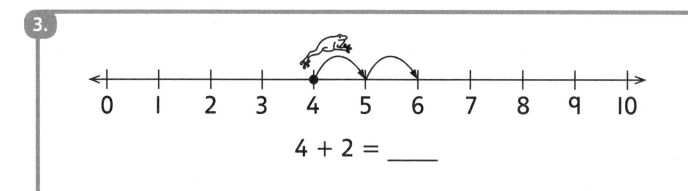

$$4 + 2 = \underline{}$$

4.

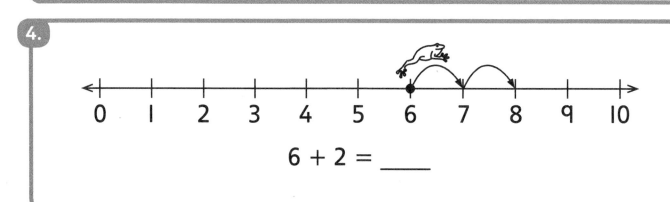

$$6 + 2 = \underline{}$$

☐ Trace the jumps.
☐ Add.

5.

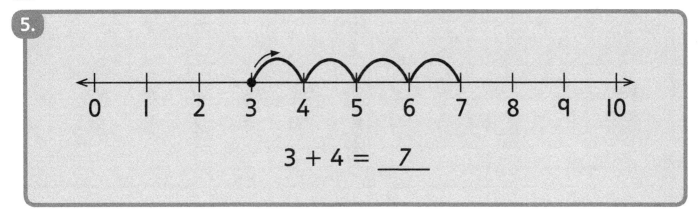

$$3 + 4 = \underline{\ 7\ }$$

6.

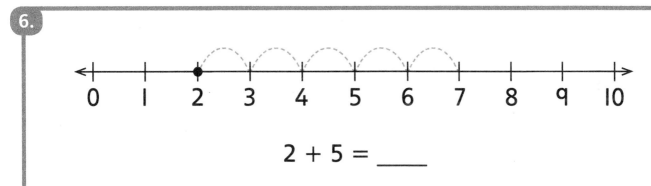

$$2 + 5 = \underline{\qquad}$$

7.

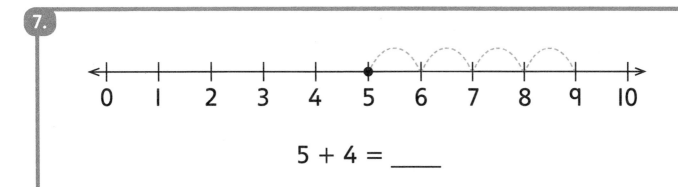

$$5 + 4 = \underline{\qquad}$$

8.

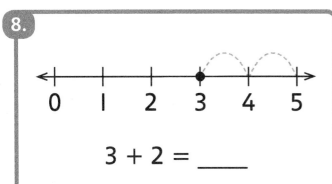

$$3 + 2 = \underline{\qquad}$$

9. BONUS

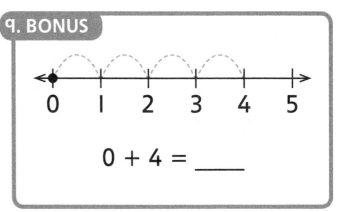

$$0 + 4 = \underline{\qquad}$$

☐ Match the dots to the addition sentence.

10.

$2 + 3 = 5$

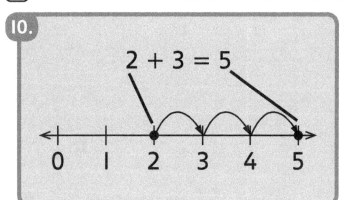

11.

$1 + 4 = 5$

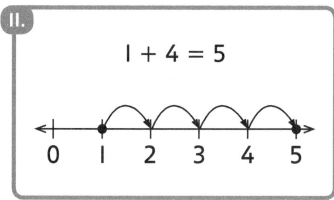

12.

$1 + 2 = 3$

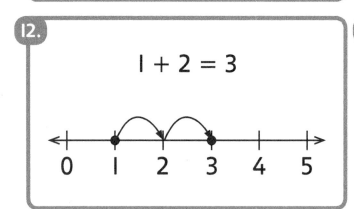

13.

$2 + 1 = 3$

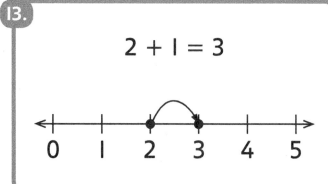

☐ Fill in the blanks.

14.

_1_ $+ 3 =$ _4_

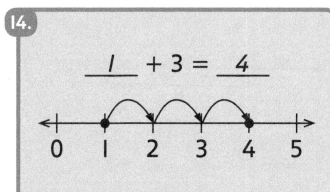

15.

____ $+ 2 =$ ____

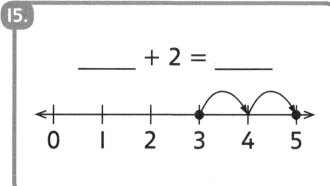

16.

____ $+ 1 =$ ____

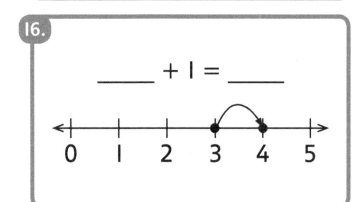

17. BONUS

____ $+ 3 =$ ____

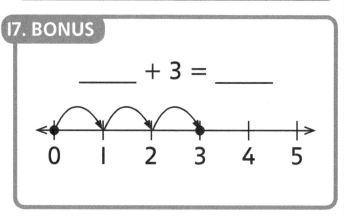

Operations and Algebraic Thinking 1-19

☐ Count the jumps.
☐ Fill in the blank.

18.
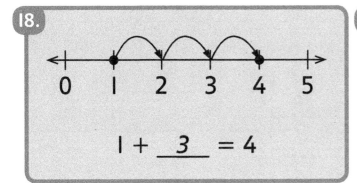

$1 + \underline{3} = 4$

19.
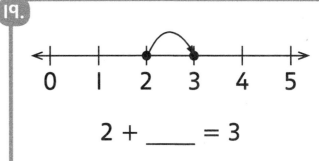

$2 + \underline{} = 3$

20.
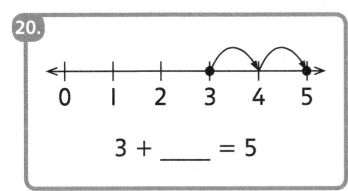

$3 + \underline{} = 5$

21.
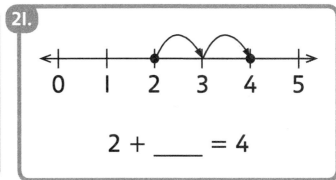

$2 + \underline{} = 4$

☐ Trace the correct number of jumps.
☐ Add.

22.
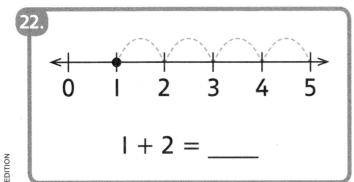

$1 + 2 = \underline{}$

23.
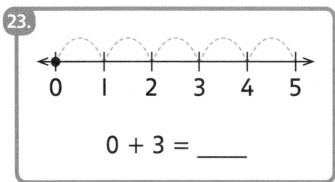

$0 + 3 = \underline{}$

24.
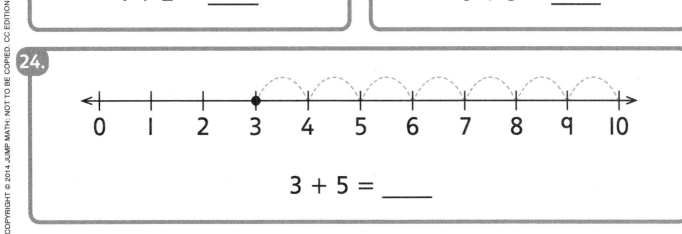

$3 + 5 = \underline{}$

☐ Use a number line to add.

25.

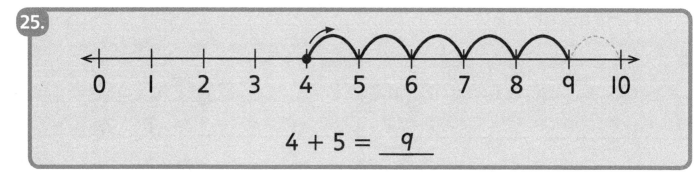

$4 + 5 =$ __q__

26.

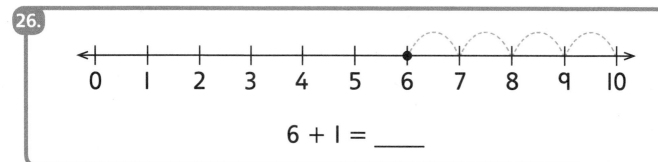

$6 + 1 =$ ____

27.

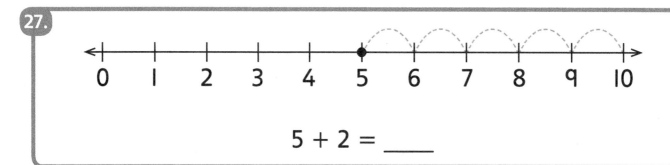

$5 + 2 =$ ____

28.

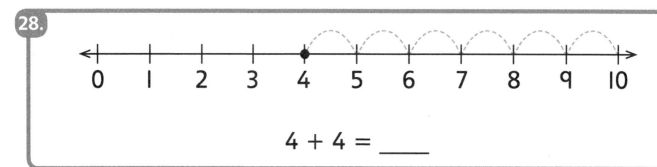

$4 + 4 =$ ____

29.

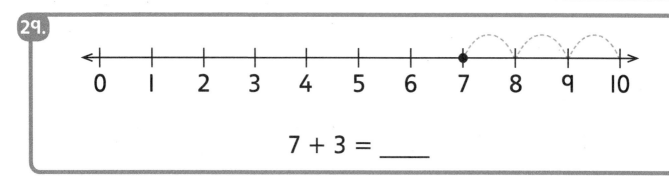

$7 + 3 =$ ____

Operations and Algebraic Thinking 1-19

OAI-20 Adding 5

☐ Count the fingers that are up.
☐ Add.

1.
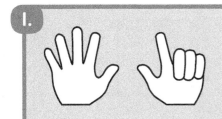

5 + 2 = _7_

2.

5 + 1 = ___

3.

5 + 3 = ___

4.

5 + 4 = ___

5.

5 + 5 = ___

6.

2 + 5 = ___

7.
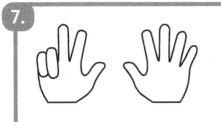

3 + 5 = ___

8.
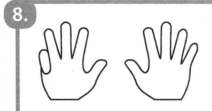

4 + 5 = ___

☐ Shade the next 5 numbers.
☐ Add 5.

9.

1	2	3	4	5
6	7	8	9	10

$4 + 5 = \underline{9}$

10.

1	2	3	4	5
6	7	8	9	10

$1 + 5 = \underline{}$

11.

1	2	3	4	5
6	7	8	9	10

$2 + 5 = \underline{}$

12.

1	2	3	4	5
6	7	8	9	10

$3 + 5 = \underline{}$

☐ Look down a row to add 5.

13.

1	2	3	4	5
6	7	8	9	10

$4 + 5 = \underline{9}$

14.

$2 + 5 = \underline{}$

15.

$5 + 5 = \underline{}$

16.

$3 + 5 = \underline{}$

17.

$1 + 5 = \underline{}$

Operations and Algebraic Thinking I-20

OAI-21 Adding 10

☐ Shade the next 10 numbers.
☐ Add 10.

1.

1	2	3	4	5	6	7	8	9	10
11	12	13	14	15	16	17	18	19	20

$$4 + 10 = \underline{\ 14\ }$$

2.

1	2	3	4	5	6	7	8	9	10
11	12	13	14	15	16	17	18	19	20

$$9 + 10 = \underline{\quad}$$

3.

1	2	3	4	5	6	7	8	9	10
11	12	13	14	15	16	17	18	19	20

$$1 + 10 = \underline{\quad}$$

4.

1	2	3	4	5	6	7	8	9	10
11	12	13	14	15	16	17	18	19	20

$$8 + 10 = \underline{\quad}$$

☐ Look down a row to add 10.

1	2	3	4	5	6	7	8	9	10
11	12	13	14	15	16	17	18	19	20

5. 2 + 10 = ____

6. 7 + 10 = ____

7. 9 + 10 = ____

8. 6 + 10 = ____

9. 1 + 10 = ____

10. 5 + 10 = ____

11. 10 + 10 = ____

12. 8 + 10 = ____

13. 3 + 10 = ____

☐ **BONUS:** Cover the rest of the page.

14. 7 + 10 = ____

15. 9 + 10 = ____

16. 4 + 10 = ____

17. 5 + 10 = ____

18. 2 + 10 = ____

19. 1 + 10 = ____

20. 6 + 10 = ____

21. 8 + 10 = ____

22. 10 + 10 = ____

Operations and Algebraic Thinking 1-21

The basket has 10 apples.
☐ How many apples are there in all?

23.

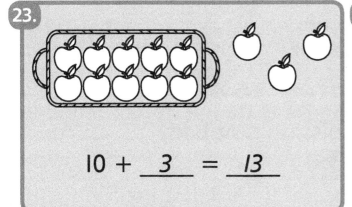

10 + __3__ = __13__

24.

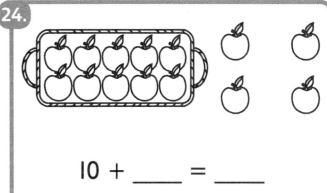

10 + ____ = ____

25.

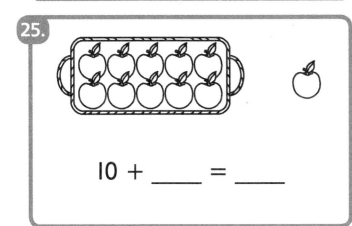

10 + ____ = ____

26.

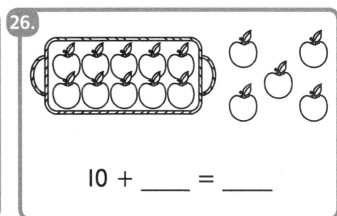

10 + ____ = ____

☐ Add.

27.

10 + 2 = ____

28.

10 + 7 = ____

29.

10 + 6 = ____

30.

10 + 8 = ____

31.

10
+ 5
___

32.

10
+ 3
___

33.

10
+ 4
___

34.

10
+ 1
___

35.

10
+ 9
___

OAI-22 Pairs That Add to 5 or 10

 3 fingers up   +   2 fingers not up   =   5 in all

 Use your fingers to find the missing number.

1. $1 + \boxed{} = 5$

2. $4 + \boxed{} = 5$

3. $\boxed{} + 3 = 5$

4. $2 + \boxed{} = 5$

5. $\boxed{} + 2 = 5$

6. $\boxed{} + 1 = 5$

7.
$$\begin{array}{r} 2 \\ + \boxed{} \\ \hline 5 \end{array}$$

8.
$$\begin{array}{r} \boxed{} \\ + \quad 1 \\ \hline 5 \end{array}$$

9.
$$\begin{array}{r} \boxed{} \\ + \quad 3 \\ \hline 5 \end{array}$$

10.
$$\begin{array}{r} 5 \\ + \boxed{} \\ \hline 5 \end{array}$$

11. BONUS $2 + 3 = \boxed{} + 4$

12. BONUS $3 + 2 = \boxed{} + 5$

13. BONUS $4 + 1 = 3 + \boxed{}$

14. BONUS $2 + \boxed{} = 4 + 1$

7	+	3	=	10
up		not up		in all

☐ Use your fingers to find the missing number.

15. $4 + \boxed{} = 10$

16. $5 + \boxed{} = 10$

17. $2 + \boxed{} = 10$

18. $\boxed{} + 7 = 10$

19. $\boxed{} + 5 = 10$

20. $\boxed{} + 1 = 10$

21.
$$\begin{array}{r} 8 \\ + \boxed{} \\ \hline 10 \end{array}$$

22.
$$\begin{array}{r} 3 \\ + \boxed{} \\ \hline 10 \end{array}$$

23.
$$\begin{array}{r} \boxed{} \\ + \quad 9 \\ \hline 10 \end{array}$$

24.
$$\begin{array}{r} 10 \\ + \boxed{} \\ \hline 10 \end{array}$$

25. BONUS
$7 + 3 = \boxed{} + 4$

26. BONUS
$2 + 8 = \boxed{} + 5$

27. BONUS
$\boxed{} + 9 = 3 + 7$

28. BONUS
$10 + \boxed{} = 6 + 4$

OAI-23 Patterns in Adding

☐ Shade the first number of hearts.
☐ Finish the addition sentence.

1. $0 + \boxed{4} = 4$

2. $1 + \boxed{} = 4$

3. $2 + \boxed{} = 4$

4. $3 + \boxed{} = 4$

5. $4 + \boxed{} = 4$

6. As the number of ♥ goes up by 1,

the number of ♡ goes _____.

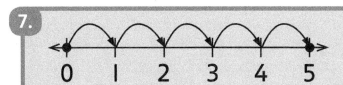

☐ Write the addition sentence.

7.

| 0 | 1 | 2 | 3 | 4 | 5 |

$\boxed{0}$ + $\boxed{5}$ = $\boxed{5}$

8.

| 0 | 1 | 2 | 3 | 4 | 5 |

$\boxed{1}$ + $\boxed{}$ = $\boxed{}$

9.

| 0 | 1 | 2 | 3 | 4 | 5 |

$\boxed{}$ + $\boxed{}$ = $\boxed{}$

10.

| 0 | 1 | 2 | 3 | 4 | 5 |

$\boxed{}$ + $\boxed{}$ = $\boxed{}$

11.

| 0 | 1 | 2 | 3 | 4 | 5 |

$\boxed{}$ + $\boxed{}$ = $\boxed{}$

12.

| 0 | 1 | 2 | 3 | 4 | 5 |

$\boxed{}$ + $\boxed{}$ = $\boxed{}$

☐ Finish the addition sentence.

13.

$\boxed{}$ + 3 = 5

14.

1 + $\boxed{}$ = 5

15.

2 + $\boxed{}$ = 5

16.

$\boxed{}$ + 5 = 5

☐ Show all the ways to make 6.
☐ Show all the ways to make 7.

17.

$0 + 6 = 6$

$1 + 5 = 6$

$\square + \square = 6$

$\square + \square = 6$

$\square + \square = 6$

$\square + \square = 6$

$\square + \square = 6$

18.

$0 + 7 = 7$

$1 + 6 = 7$

$\square + \square = 7$

$\square + \square = 7$

$\square + \square = 7$

$\square + \square = 7$

$\square + \square = 7$

$\square + \square = 7$

☐ Finish the addition sentence.

19.

$3 + \square = 7$

20.

$2 + \square = 6$

21.

$\square + 5 = 6$

22.

$\square + 1 = 7$

Operations and Algebraic Thinking 1-23

☐ Show all the ways to make 8.
☐ Show all the ways to make 9.

23.

$0 + 8 = 8$

$1 + 7 = 8$

$\square + \square = 8$

$\square + \square = 8$

$\square + \square = 8$

$\square + \square = 8$

$\square + \square = 8$

$\square + \square = 8$

$\square + \square = 8$

24.

$0 + 9 = 9$

$1 + 8 = 9$

$\square + \square = 9$

$\square + \square = 9$

$\square + \square = 9$

$\square + \square = 9$

$\square + \square = 9$

$\square + \square = 9$

$\square + \square = 9$

$\square + \square = 9$

☐ Finish the addition sentence.

25.

$4 + \square = 9$

26.

$\square + 3 = 8$

OAI-24 Adding 3 Numbers

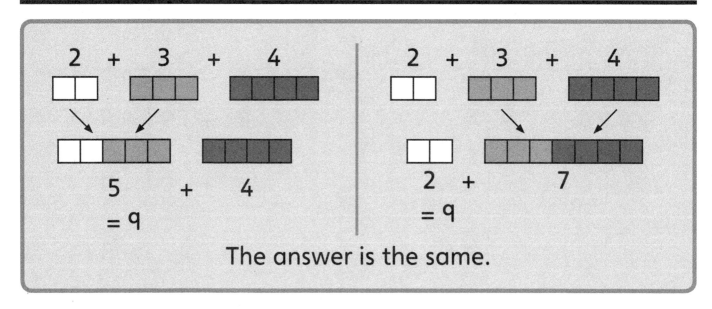

2 + 3 + 4

5 + 4
= 9

2 + 3 + 4

2 + 7
= 9

The answer is the same.

☐ Add the circled numbers.
☐ Copy the last number.

1. ③ + ② + 1

＿5＿ + ＿1＿

2. ③ + ① + 3

＿＿ + ＿＿

3. ④ + ① + 2

＿＿ + ＿＿

4. ③ + ③ + 4

＿＿ + ＿＿

5. ① + ② + 2

＿＿ + ＿＿

6. ② + ② + 3

＿＿ + ＿＿

7. ③ + ① + 1

＿＿ + ＿＿

8. ④ + ① + 4

＿＿ + ＿＿

☐ Copy the first number.
☐ Add the circled numbers.

9.
$$3 + ⑦ + ①$$
$$\underline{\ 3\ } + \underline{\ 8\ }$$

10.
$$2 + ② + ④$$
$$\underline{\ \ \ \ } + \underline{\ \ \ \ }$$

11.
$$4 + ③ + ③$$
$$\underline{\ \ \ \ } + \underline{\ \ \ \ }$$

12.
$$5 + ③ + ②$$
$$\underline{\ \ \ \ } + \underline{\ \ \ \ }$$

13.
$$6 + ④ + ①$$
$$\underline{\ \ \ \ } + \underline{\ \ \ \ }$$

14.
$$2 + ① + ⑤$$
$$\underline{\ \ \ \ } + \underline{\ \ \ \ }$$

☐ Add the circled numbers. Find the answer.

15.
$$③ + ② + 4$$
$$\underline{\ 5\ } + \underline{\ 4\ } = \underline{\ 9\ }$$

16.
$$3 + ② + ④$$
$$\underline{\ 3\ } + \underline{\ 6\ } = \underline{\ 9\ }$$

17.
$$⑤ + ① + 3$$
$$\underline{\ \ \ \ } + \underline{\ 3\ } = \underline{\ \ \ \ }$$

18.
$$5 + ① + ③$$
$$\underline{\ 5\ } + \underline{\ \ \ \ } = \underline{\ \ \ \ }$$

19.
$$③ + ② + 1$$
$$\underline{\ \ \ \ } + \underline{\ \ \ \ } = \underline{\ \ \ \ }$$

20.
$$3 + ② + ①$$
$$\underline{\ \ \ \ } + \underline{\ \ \ \ } = \underline{\ \ \ \ }$$

OAI-25 Using 5 to Add

☐ Circle two numbers that add to 5.

1.
② ③ 4

2.
1   3   4

3.
1   2   3

4.
1   2   4

5.
4   1   3

6.
3   4   2

☐ Circle two numbers that add to 5.
☐ Write the number that is left over.

7.
② + ③ + 4 = 5 + ☐4

8.
4 + 1 + 3 = 5 + ☐

9.
3 + 1 + 4 = 5 + ☐

10.
0 + 3 + 5 = 5 + ☐

11.
4 + 3 + 2 = 5 + ☐

☐ Circle two numbers that add to 5.

☐ Use 5 to add.

12.

$(4) + (1) + 3$

$= 5 + \boxed{3}$

$= \boxed{8}$

13.

$3 + (1) + (4)$

$= 5 + \square$

$= \square$

14.

$2 + 3 + 4$

$= 5 + \square$

$= \square$

15.

$3 + 4 + 2$

$= 5 + \square$

$= \square$

16.

$2 + 4 + 3$

$= 5 + \square$

$= \square$

17.

$3 + 1 + 2$

$= 5 + \square$

$= \square$

18.

$1 + 2 + 3$

$= 5 + \square$

$= \square$

19.

$2 + 1 + 4$

$= 5 + \square$

$= \square$

20.

$4 + 3 + 1$

$= 5 + \square$

$= \square$

21.

$4 + 3 + 2 = \square$

22.

$4 + 2 + 1 = \square$

23.

$3 + 2 + 1 = \square$

24.

$3 + 4 + 1 = \square$

OAI-26 Using 10 to Add

☐ Circle two numbers that add to 10.

1. 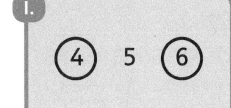 ④ 5 ⑥

2. 3 7 9

3. 1 8 9

4. 4 5 5

5. 2 3 8

6. 3 6 4

☐ Circle two numbers that add to 10.
☐ Write the number that is left over.

7. ⑧ + ② + 5 = 10 + 5

8. 4 + 6 + 3 = 10 + ☐

9. 2 + 9 + 1 = 10 + ☐

10. 6 + 7 + 4 = 10 + ☐

11. 4 + 3 + 7 = 10 + ☐

◯ Circle two numbers that add to 10.

◯ Use 10 to add.

12.

$(8) + 3 + (2)$

$= 10 + \boxed{3}$

$= \boxed{13}$

13.

$2 + (7) + (3)$

$= 10 + \boxed{}$

$= \boxed{}$

14.

$1 + 8 + 9$

$= 10 + \boxed{}$

$= \boxed{}$

15.

$3 + 7 + 4$

$= 10 + \boxed{}$

$= \boxed{}$

16.

$4 + 5 + 6$

$= 10 + \boxed{}$

$= \boxed{}$

17.

$5 + 5 + 6$

$= 10 + \boxed{}$

$= \boxed{}$

18.

$9 + 2 + 1$

$= 10 + \boxed{}$

$= \boxed{}$

19.

$3 + 2 + 8$

$= 10 + \boxed{}$

$= \boxed{}$

20.

$4 + 5 + 5$

$= 10 + \boxed{}$

$= \boxed{}$

21.

$8 + 4 + 2$

$= 10 + \boxed{}$

$= \boxed{}$

22.

$7 + 3 + 9$

$= 10 + \boxed{}$

$= \boxed{}$

23.

$6 + 4 + 8$

$= 10 + \boxed{}$

$= \boxed{}$

OAI-27 **Doubles**

☐ Write a doubles sentence.

1.

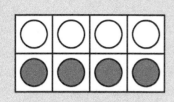

4 + 4 = __8__

2.

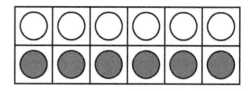

6 + 6 = ____

3.

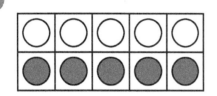

5 + 5 = ____

4.

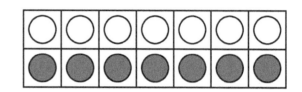

7 + 7 = ____

5.

2 + 2 = ____

6.

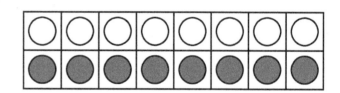

8 + 8 = ____

7.

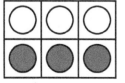

3 + 3 = ____

8.

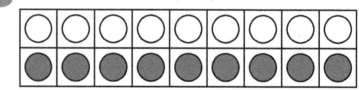

q + q = ____

Operations and Algebraic Thinking I-27

☐ Draw circles to double the number.

9.

Double 3 is __6__.

3 + 3 = ____

10.

Double 4 is ____.

4 + 4 = ____

11.

Double 2 is ____.

2 + 2 = ____

12.

Double 5 is ____.

5 + 5 = ____

13.

Double 8 is ____.

8 + 8 = ____

14.

Double 7 is ____.

7 + 7 = ____

☐ Fill in the boxes.

15.

$1 + 1 =$ ☐

$2 + 2 =$ ☐

$3 + 3 =$ ☐

$4 + 4 =$ ☐

$5 + 5 =$ ☐

$6 + 6 =$ ☐

$7 + 7 =$ ☐

$8 + 8 =$ ☐

$9 + 9 =$ ☐

$10 + 10 =$ ☐

☐ Fill in the blanks.

16.

Tim has 2 cats.

Jane has 2 cats.

They have ____ + ____ = ____ cats altogether.

17.

Sun has 4 blocks.

Bill has 4 blocks.

They have ____ + ____ = ____ blocks altogether.

OAI-28 Using Doubles to Add

☐ Fill in the blanks.

1.

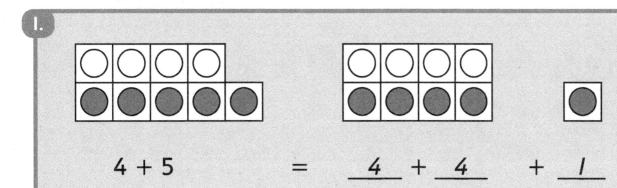

$$4 + 5 \quad = \quad \underline{4} + \underline{4} + \underline{1}$$

2.

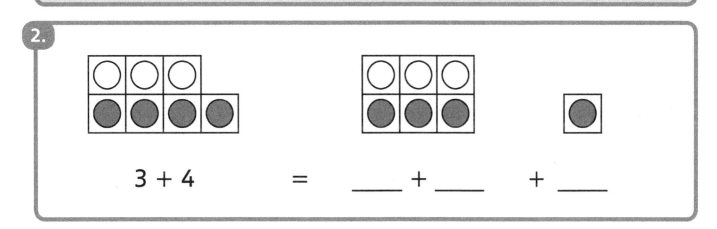

$$3 + 4 \quad = \quad \underline{} + \underline{} + \underline{}$$

3.

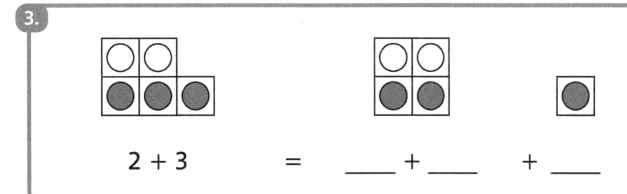

$$2 + 3 \quad = \quad \underline{} + \underline{} + \underline{}$$

4.

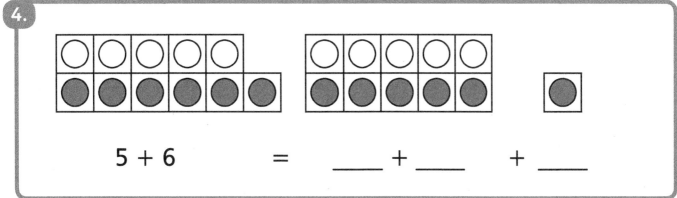

$$5 + 6 \quad = \quad \underline{} + \underline{} + \underline{}$$

☐ Circle the smaller number.
☐ Write the double of the smaller number and add I.

5.
5 + ④
= _4_ + _4_ + _I_

6.
⑤ + 6
= _5_ + _5_ + _I_

7.
3 + 4
= ___ + ___ + ___

8.
8 + 7
= ___ + ___ + ___

9.
7 + 6
= ___ + ___ + ___

10.
4 + 3
= ___ + ___ + ___

☐ Fill in the blanks.

11.
4 + 5
= 4 + 4 + I
= ___ + I
= ___

12.
6 + 7
= 6 + 6 + I
= ___ + I
= ___

☐ Add.

13. 3 + 4

14. 6 + 5

15. 8 + 9

16. 7 + 8

Operations and Algebraic Thinking I-28

☐ Fill in the doubles.

1.

1 + 1 = __2__	6 + 6 = __12__
2 + 2 = __4__	7 + 7 = __14__
3 + 3 = __6__	8 + 8 = ____
4 + 4 = ____	9 + 9 = ____
5 + 5 = ____	10 + 10 = ____

Remember: 6 + 7 = 6 + 6 + 1 = 12 + 1 = 13

☐ Write a double plus I.

☐ Add.

2.

5 + 6 = __5__ + __5__ + __1__	5 + 6 = ____
4 + 5 = ____ + ____ + ____	4 + 5 = ____
7 + 8 = ____ + ____ + ____	7 + 8 = ____
8 + 9 = ____ + ____ + ____	8 + 9 = ____

☐ Add.

3.

John has 5 fish. Kate has 4 fish.

They have ____ + ____ = ____ fish altogether.

☐ Circle doubles or numbers that add to 10.
☐ Find the answer.

4.
(5) + 2 + (5)

_10_ + _2_ = _12_

5.
6 + 3 + 4

___ + ___ = ___

6.
7 + 3 + 9

___ + ___ = ___

7.
6 + 6 + 2

___ + ___ = ___

8.
2 + 6 + 8

___ + ___ = ___

9.
8 + 3 + 8

___ + ___ = ___

10.
4 + 6 + 9

___ + ___ = ___

11.
4 + 7 + 3

___ + ___ = ___

12.
8 + 5 + 5

___ + ___ = ___

13.
9 + 7 + 1

___ + ___ = ___

14.
6 + 7

15.
8 + 4 + 2

16.
6 + 6 + 1

17.
9 + 1 + 6

Operations and Algebraic Thinking 1-29

OAI-30 Addition Word Problems

☐ Add. Use the pictures to help you.

1. 3 + 2 = ☐

3 flowers  2 more flowers

2. 5 + 3 = ☐

5 flowers 3 more flowers

3. 4 + 4 = ☐

4 flowers 4 more flowers

4. 3 + 6 = ☐

3 flowers 6 more flowers

5. 2 + 5 = ☐

2 flowers 5 more flowers

☐ Draw a picture to add.
☐ Write the number sentence.

6.

2 trees   7 more trees

     🌳🌳🌳🌳🌳🌳🌳

| 2 | + | 7 | = | 9 |

7.

5 pencils   4 more pencils

☐ + ☐ = ☐

8.

6 baseballs   5 more baseballs

☐ + ☐ = ☐

☐ Draw circles to help you add.

9. 3 flies are buzzing. 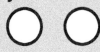 2 join them.

○ ○ ○   ○ ○

How many flies altogether?

3 + 2 = ⟦5⟧

10. Emma has 4 cats.   John has 2 cats.

How many cats altogether?

4 + 2 = ☐

11. Rob has 5 oranges.   Tina has 3 oranges.

How many oranges altogether?

☐ + ☐ = ☐

12. Sara has 4 fish.   Tom has 4 fish.

How many fish altogether?

☐ + ☐ = ☐

☐ Draw circles to solve the problem.

13.

There are 5 small turtles.

There are 6 big turtles.

How many turtles are there altogether?

☐ + ☐ = ☐

14.

8 children are playing soccer.

5 children join them.

How many are playing soccer now?

☐ + ☐ = ☐

15.

There are 7 big tables.

There are 6 small tables.

How many tables are there altogether?

☐ + ☐ = ☐

OAI-3I Subtracting

☐ Take away.

1.

$$5 - 1 = \underline{\ 4\ }$$

2.

$$4 - 1 = \underline{\qquad}$$

3.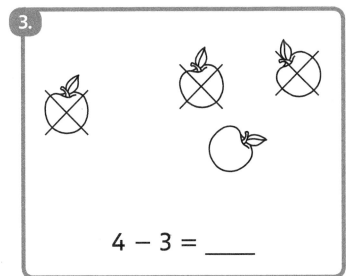

$$4 - 3 = \underline{\qquad}$$

4.

$$5 - 2 = \underline{\qquad}$$

5.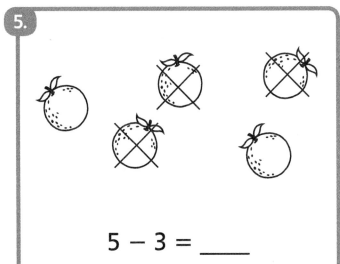

$$5 - 3 = \underline{\qquad}$$

6.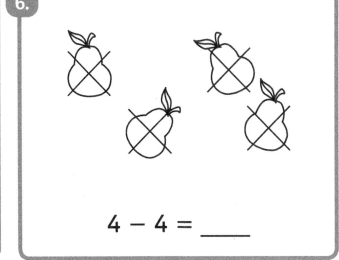

$$4 - 4 = \underline{\qquad}$$

☐ Cross out the correct number.

☐ Subtract.

7.

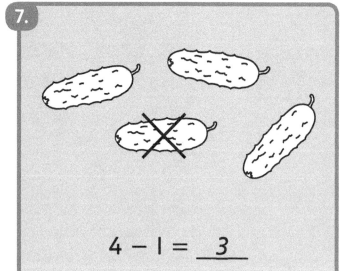

$4 - 1 = \underline{\ 3\ }$

8.

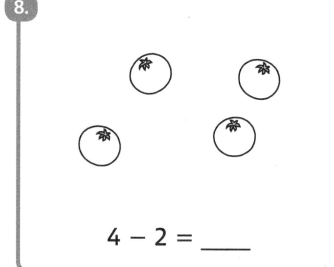

$4 - 2 = \underline{\ \ \ \ }$

9.

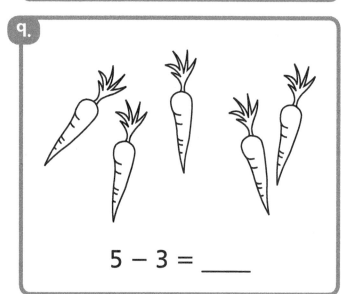

$5 - 3 = \underline{\ \ \ \ }$

10.

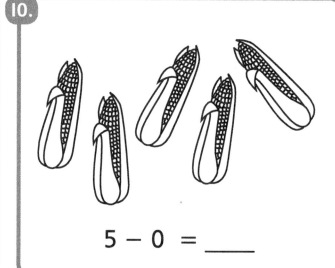

$5 - 0 = \underline{\ \ \ \ }$

11.

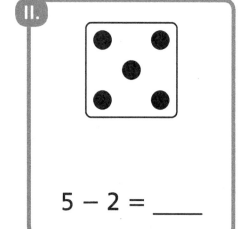

$5 - 2 = \underline{\ \ \ \ }$

12.

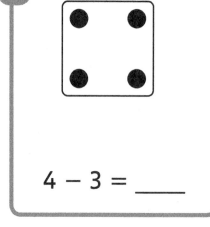

$4 - 3 = \underline{\ \ \ \ }$

13.

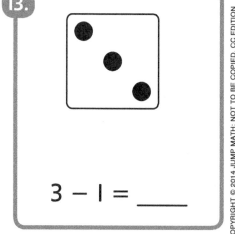

$3 - 1 = \underline{\ \ \ \ }$

☐ Draw the first number of circles.
☐ Cross out the second number of circles.
☐ Subtract.

14.
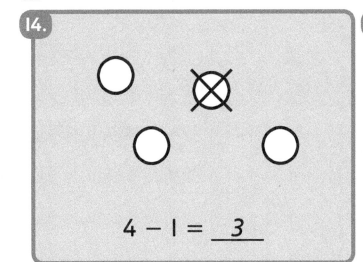
$4 - 1 = \underline{\ 3\ }$

15.
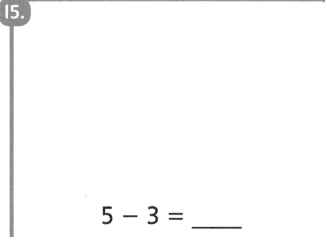
$5 - 3 = \underline{\hspace{1.5em}}$

16.
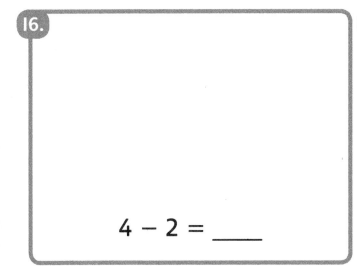
$4 - 2 = \underline{\hspace{1.5em}}$

17.
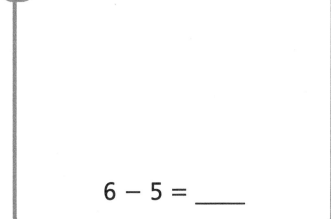
$6 - 5 = \underline{\hspace{1.5em}}$

18.
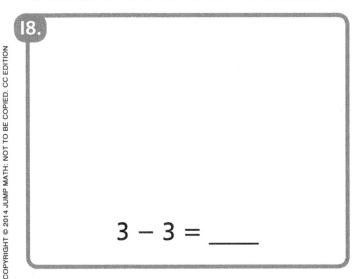
$3 - 3 = \underline{\hspace{1.5em}}$

19.
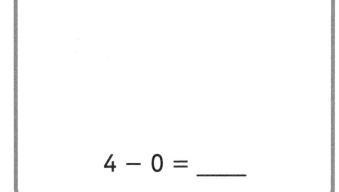
$4 - 0 = \underline{\hspace{1.5em}}$

Eric has 10 apples.

Kim takes away 4 apples.

☐ How many are left?

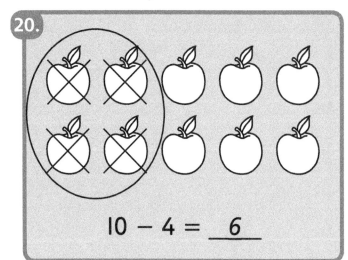

20.

$10 - 4 = \underline{6}$

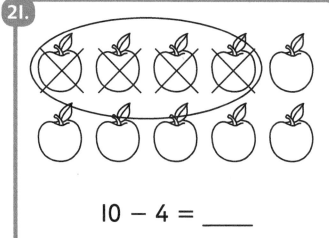

21.

$10 - 4 = \underline{}$

22.

$10 - 4 = \underline{}$

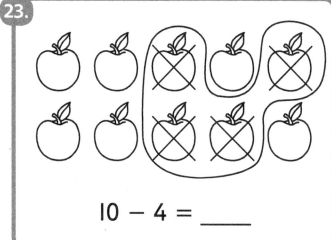

23.

$10 - 4 = \underline{}$

☐ Take away any 4 apples.

☐ How many are left?

24.

$10 - 4 = \underline{}$

OAI-32 Subtracting 1 or 2

☐ Take away the last circle.
☐ Subtract 1.

1.

    1   2   3   4

    ○ ○ ○ ⊗

$4 - 1 = \underline{\ \ 3\ \ }$

2.

   1   2   3   4   5

   ○ ○ ○ ○ ⊗

$5 - 1 = \underline{\ \ \ \ }$

3.

   1   2   3   4   5   6

   ○ ○ ○ ○ ○ ○

$6 - 1 = \underline{\ \ \ \ }$

4.

   1   2   3   4   5   6   7

   ○ ○ ○ ○ ○ ○ ○

$7 - 1 = \underline{\ \ \ \ }$

5.

   1   2   3   4   5   6   7   8   9   10

   ○ ○ ○ ○ ○ ○ ○ ○ ○ ○

$10 - 1 = \underline{\ \ \ \ }$

6.

   1   2   3   4   5   6   7   8

   ○ ○ ○ ○ ○ ○ ○ ○

$8 - 1 = \underline{\ \ \ \ }$

◻ Take away 2 boxes.
◻ Subtract 2.

7.

1	2	3	4	5	☒	☒

$7 - 2 = \underline{\ 5\ }$

8.

1	2	3	4	5	6

$6 - 2 = \underline{\ \ \ }$

9.

1	2	3	4	5	6	7	8

$8 - 2 = \underline{\ \ \ }$

10.

1	2	3	4	5

$5 - 2 = \underline{\ \ \ }$

11.

1	2	3	4	5	6	7	8	9

$9 - 2 = \underline{\ \ \ }$

Operations and Algebraic Thinking 1-32

☐ Start at the big dot. Draw I jump back.
☐ Subtract I.

12.

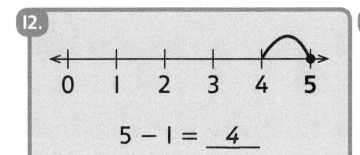

$$5 - 1 = \underline{\ \ 4\ \ }$$

13.

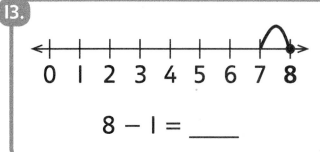

$$8 - 1 = \underline{\ \ \ \ \ }$$

14.

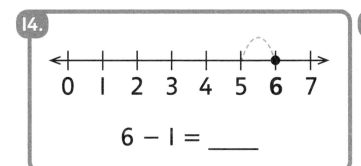

$$6 - 1 = \underline{\ \ \ \ \ }$$

15.

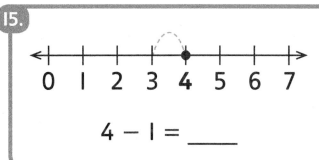

$$4 - 1 = \underline{\ \ \ \ \ }$$

16.

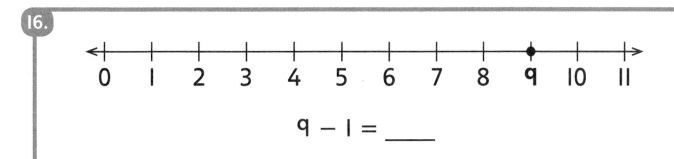

$$9 - 1 = \underline{\ \ \ \ \ }$$

17.

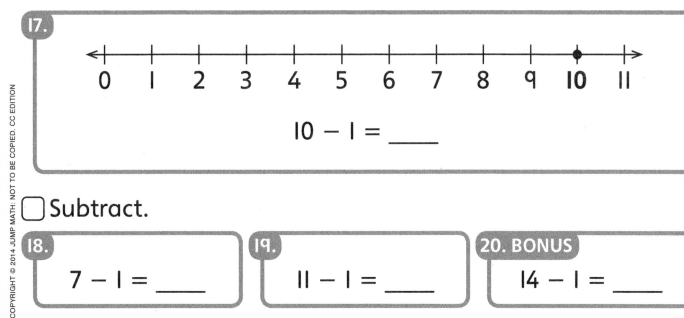

$$10 - 1 = \underline{\ \ \ \ \ }$$

☐ Subtract.

18.

$$7 - 1 = \underline{\ \ \ \ \ }$$

19.

$$11 - 1 = \underline{\ \ \ \ \ }$$

20. BONUS

$$14 - 1 = \underline{\ \ \ \ \ }$$

☐ Draw 2 jumps back.
☐ Subtract 2.

21.

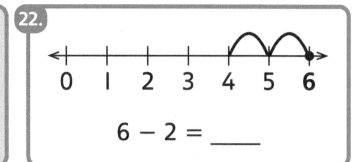

5 − 2 = __3__

22.

6 − 2 = ____

23.

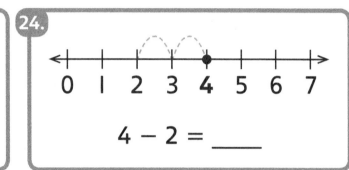

7 − 2 = ____

24.

4 − 2 = ____

25.

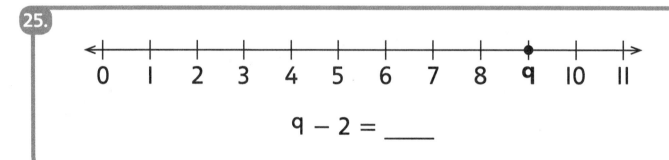

9 − 2 = ____

26.

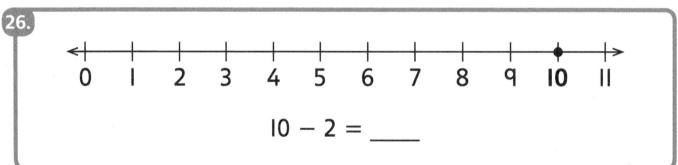

10 − 2 = ____

☐ Subtract.

27.

8 − 2 = ____

28.

11 − 2 = ____

29. BONUS

15 − 2 = ____

Operations and Algebraic Thinking I-32

OAI-33 Using Number Lines to Subtract

◻ Trace the jumps. Start at the big dot.

◻ Count the jumps.

1.

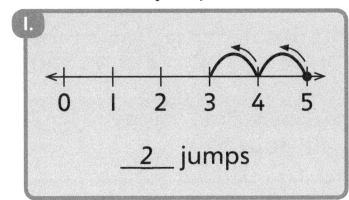

__2__ jumps

2.

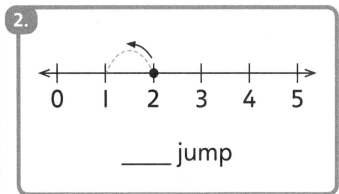

____ jump

3.

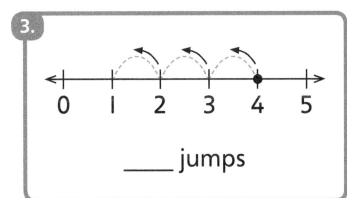

____ jumps

4.

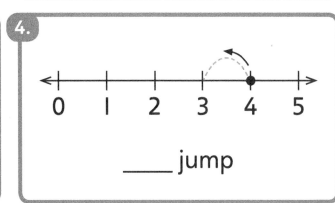

____ jump

5.

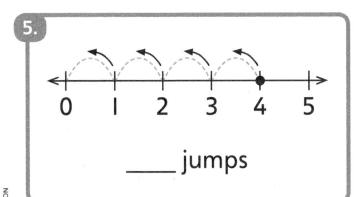

____ jumps

6.

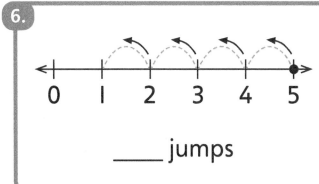

____ jumps

7.

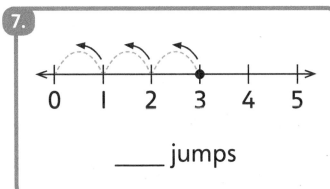

____ jumps

8.

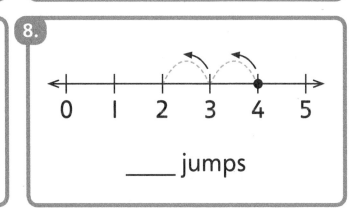

____ jumps

☐ Fill in the blanks.

9.

The frog takes __3__ jumps.

It stops at __1__.

10.

The frog takes __2__ jumps.

It stops at ____.

11.

The frog takes ____ jumps.

It stops at ____.

12.

The frog takes ____ jump.

It stops at ____.

13.

The frog takes ____ jumps.

It stops at ____.

14.

The frog takes ____ jumps.

It stops at ____.

15.

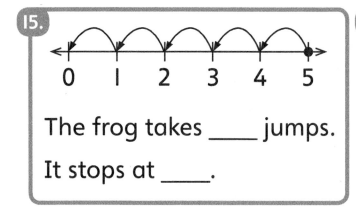

The frog takes ____ jumps.

It stops at ____.

16.

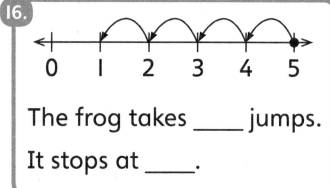

The frog takes ____ jumps.

It stops at ____.

Operations and Algebraic Thinking I-33

The frog takes 2 jumps backward.
⬜ Trace 2 jumps.
⬜ What number does the frog stop at?

17.

The frog stops at __1__.

18.

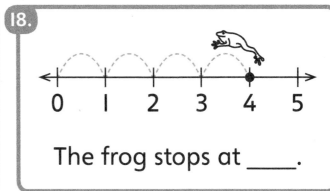

The frog stops at ____.

19.

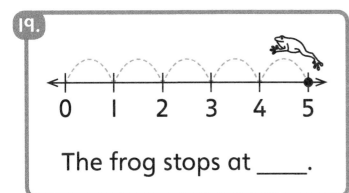

The frog stops at ____.

20.

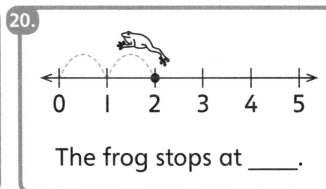

The frog stops at ____.

21.

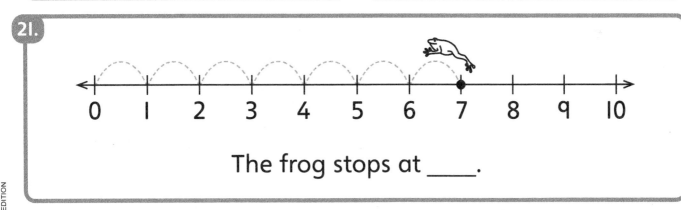

The frog stops at ____.

22.

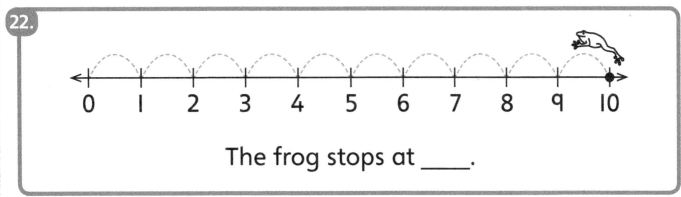

The frog stops at ____.

The frog starts at 9.

☐ How many jumps does the frog take?

23. 9 – 4

_4_ jumps

24. 9 – 3

____ jumps

25. 9 – 6

____ jumps

26. 9 – 5

____ jumps

27. 9 – 8

____ jumps

28. 9 – 1

____ jump

☐ How many jumps does the frog take?
☐ Trace the jumps.

29. 5 – 2

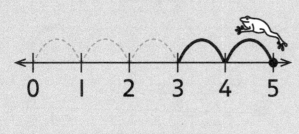

_2_ jumps

30. 4 – 3

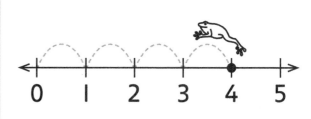

____ jumps

31. 3 – 1

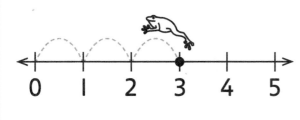

____ jump

32. 5 – 4

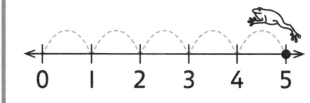

____ jumps

Operations and Algebraic Thinking 1-33

☐ Trace 4 jumps back. Start at the big dot.
☐ Subtract 4.

33.

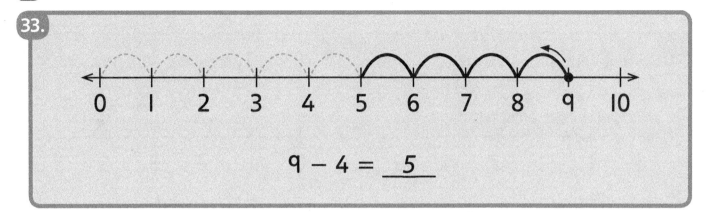

9 − 4 = __5__

34.

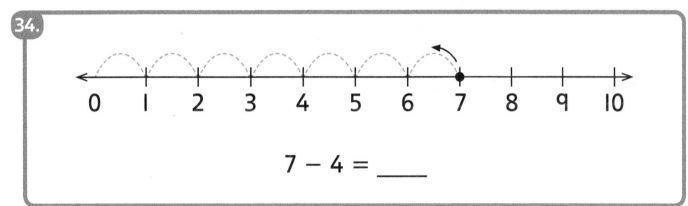

7 − 4 = ____

35.

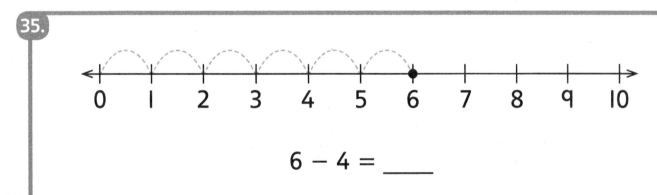

6 − 4 = ____

36.

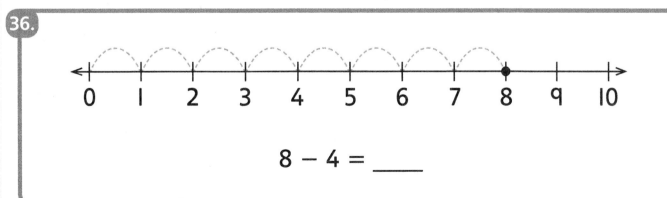

8 − 4 = ____

OAI-34 Using Number Lines to Subtract (Advanced)

☐ Trace the jumps. Start at the big dot.
☐ Fill in the blanks.

1.

3 − 2   __2__ jumps

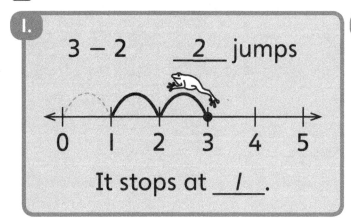

It stops at __1__.

2.

4 − 1   ____ jump

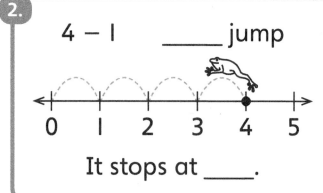

It stops at ____.

3.

5 − 3   ____ jumps

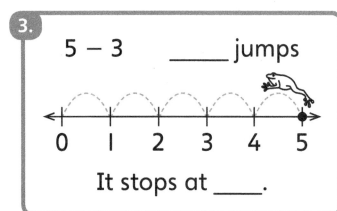

It stops at ____.

4.

5 − 4   ____ jumps

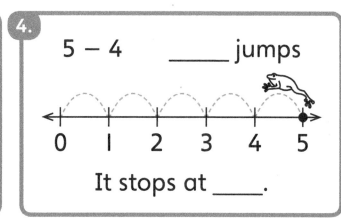

It stops at ____.

5.

9 − 4   ____ jumps

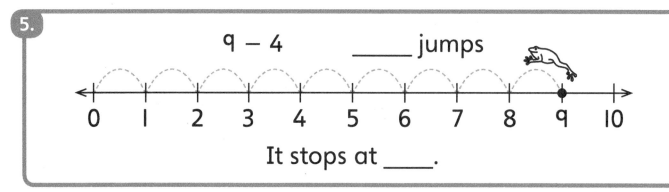

It stops at ____.

6.

10 − 3   ____ jumps

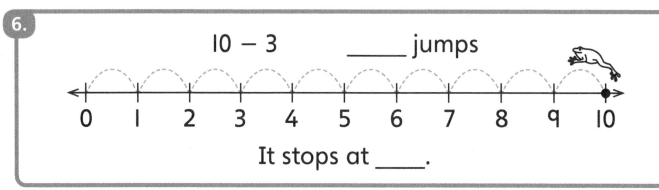

It stops at ____.

☐ Trace the jumps back. Start at the big dot.
☐ Subtract.

7.

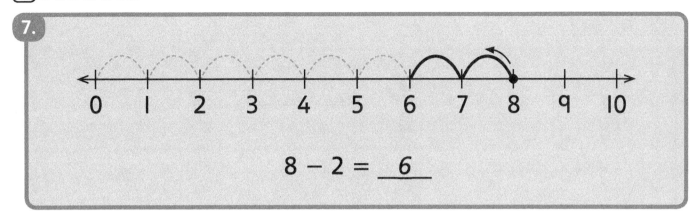

$$8 - 2 = \underline{\ 6\ }$$

8.

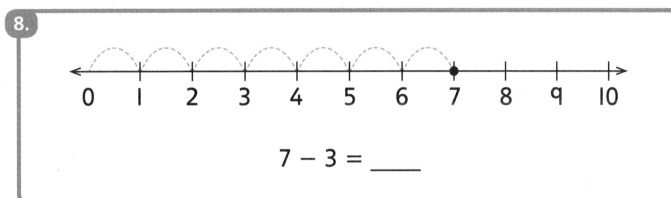

$$7 - 3 = \underline{\ \ \ \ }$$

9.

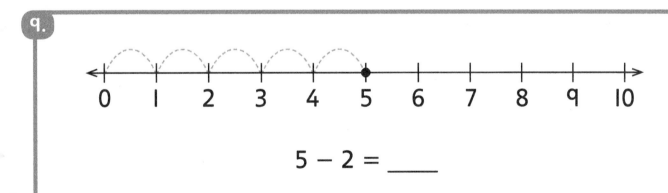

$$5 - 2 = \underline{\ \ \ \ }$$

10.

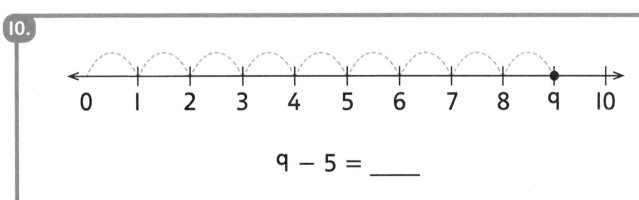

$$9 - 5 = \underline{\ \ \ \ }$$

☐ Show where to start tracing.
☐ Trace 5 jumps back.
☐ Subtract.

11.

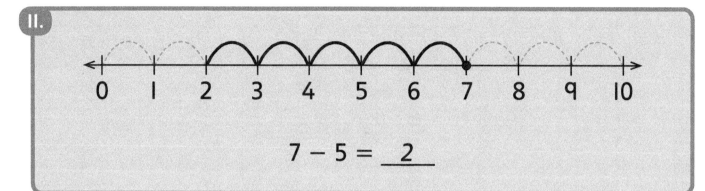

$7 - 5 = \underline{\ 2\ }$

12.

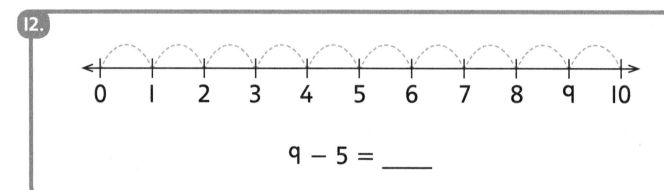

$9 - 5 = \underline{\ \ \ \ }$

13.

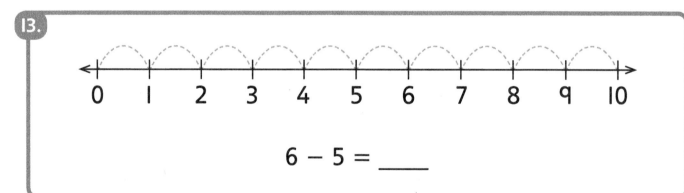

$6 - 5 = \underline{\ \ \ \ }$

14.

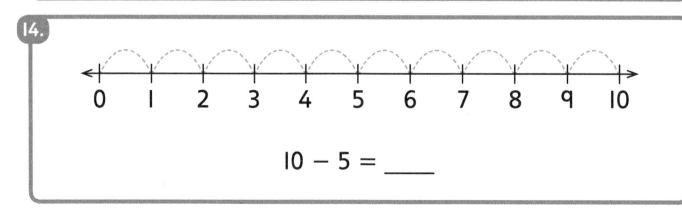

$10 - 5 = \underline{\ \ \ \ }$

Operations and Algebraic Thinking 1-34

☐ Show where to start tracing.
☐ Trace the jumps back.
☐ Subtract.

15.

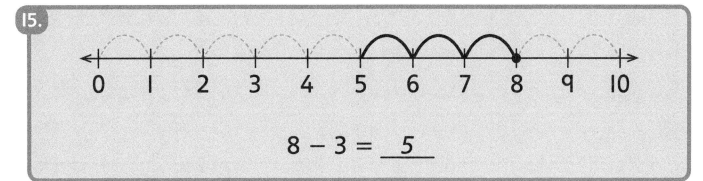

$$8 - 3 = \underline{\ 5\ }$$

16.

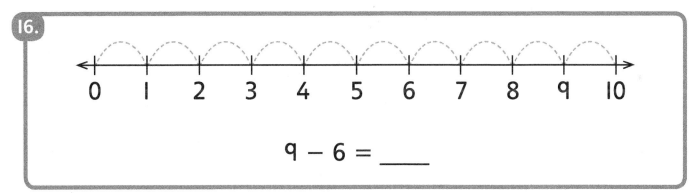

$$9 - 6 = \underline{\hphantom{000}}$$

17.

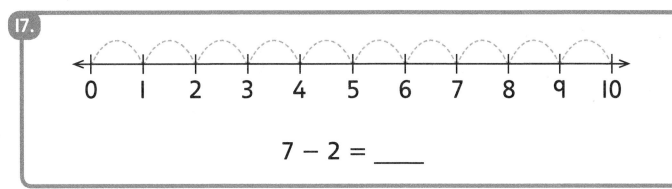

$$7 - 2 = \underline{\hphantom{000}}$$

☐ Now write the answer on the left.

18.

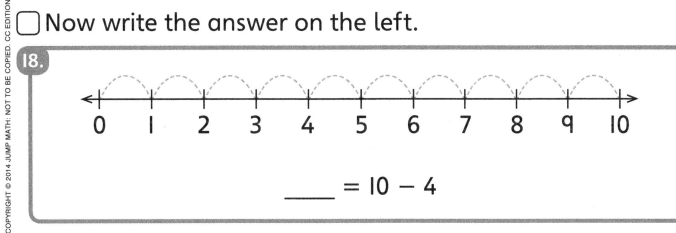

$$\underline{\hphantom{000}} = 10 - 4$$

☐ Add or subtract using the number line.

19.
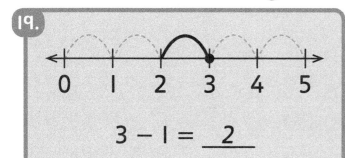

$3 - 1 = \underline{2}$

20.
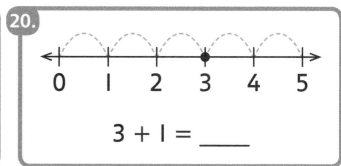

$3 + 1 = \underline{}$

21.
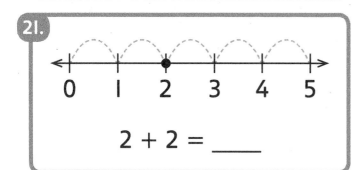

$2 + 2 = \underline{}$

22.
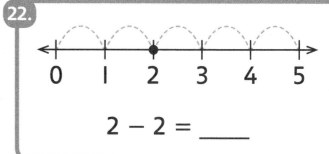

$2 - 2 = \underline{}$

23.
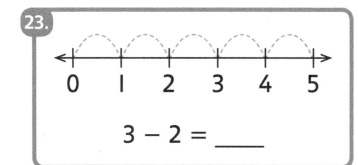

$3 - 2 = \underline{}$

24.
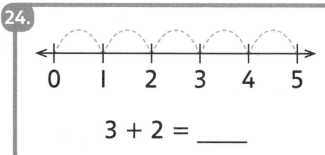

$3 + 2 = \underline{}$

25.
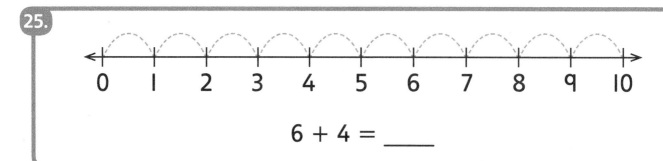

$6 + 4 = \underline{}$

26.
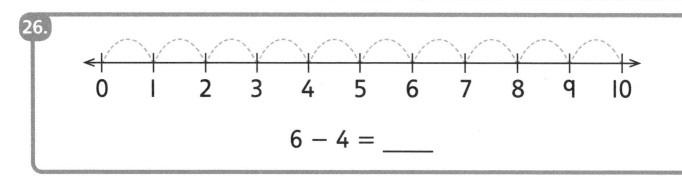

$6 - 4 = \underline{}$

Operations and Algebraic Thinking 1-34

OAI-35 Counting Back

☐ Write the number that comes **after**.

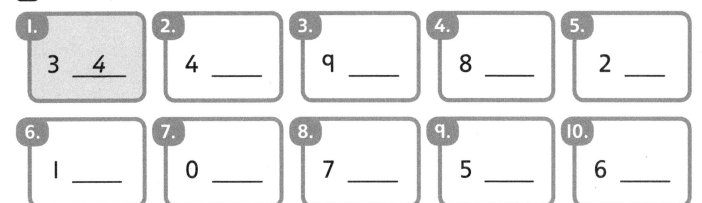

1.	2.	3.	4.	5.
3 4	4 ___	9 ___	8 ___	2 ___

6.	7.	8.	9.	10.
1 ___	0 ___	7 ___	5 ___	6 ___

☐ Write the number that comes **before**.

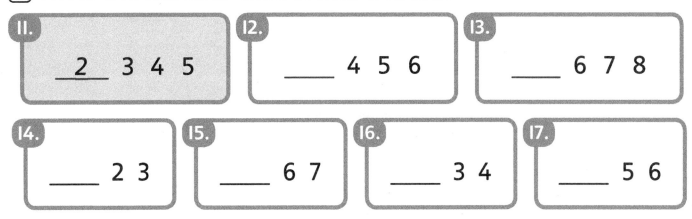

11.	12.	13.
_2_ 3 4 5	___ 4 5 6	___ 6 7 8

14.	15.	16.	17.
___ 2 3	___ 6 7	___ 3 4	___ 5 6

☐ Write the number that comes **after**.
☐ Write the number that comes **before**.

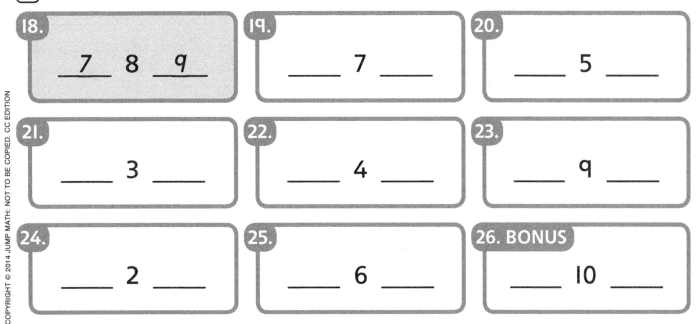

18.	19.	20.
_7_ 8 _9_	___ 7 ___	___ 5 ___

21.	22.	23.
___ 3 ___	___ 4 ___	___ 9 ___

24.	25.	26. BONUS
___ 2 ___	___ 6 ___	___ 10 ___

☐ Write the number that comes before.

27.
_7_ 8 9

28.
___ 4 5

29.
___ 2 3

30.
___ 18 19

31.
___ 14 15

32.
___ 12 13

33.
___ 16 17

34.
___ 11 12

35.
___ 19 20

☐ Write the number that comes before.
☐ Write the number that comes after.

36.
___ 15 ___

37.
___ 17 ___

38.
___ 11 ___

39.
___ 19 ___

40.
___ 12 ___

41.
___ 18 ___

42.
___ 16 ___

43.
___ 13 ___

44.
___ 14 ___

☐ **BONUS:** Fill in the blanks.

45.
___ ___ ___ 14 15 16 ___ ___ ___

Operations and Algebraic Thinking 1-35

OAI-36 Counting Back to Subtract

☐ Subtract by counting back.

1.

5   _4_   _3_

5 − 2 = _3_

2.

4   ___   ___   ___

4 − 3 = ___

3.

6   ___ ___ ___

6 − 4 = ___

4.

7   ___ ___ ___

7 − 3 = ___

5.

8   ___ ___

8 − 2 = ___

6.

5 − 3 = ___

7.

6 − 3 = ___

8.

7 − 4 = ___

OAI-37 Addition and Subtraction

$$7 \quad = \quad 4 \quad + \quad 3$$

□□□□   ▦▦▦

So $7 - 4 = 3$ and $7 - 3 = 4$

☒☒☒☒▦▦▦   □□□□☒☒☒

☐ Write two subtraction facts for the addition fact.

1.
$$7 = 5 + 2$$
So $7 - \underline{\ 2\ } = \underline{\ 5\ }$
and $7 - \underline{\ 5\ } = \underline{\ 2\ }$

2.
$$6 = 4 + 2$$
So $6 - \underline{\ \ \ \ } = \underline{\ \ \ \ }$
and $6 - \underline{\ \ \ \ } = \underline{\ \ \ \ }$

3.
$$8 = 5 + 3$$
So $8 - \underline{\ \ \ \ } = \underline{\ \ \ \ }$
and $8 - \underline{\ \ \ \ } = \underline{\ \ \ \ }$

4.
$$9 = 3 + 6$$
So $9 - \underline{\ \ \ \ } = \underline{\ \ \ \ }$
and $9 - \underline{\ \ \ \ } = \underline{\ \ \ \ }$

5.
$$10 = 6 + 4$$
So $10 - \underline{\ \ \ \ } = \underline{\ \ \ \ }$
and $10 - \underline{\ \ \ \ } = \underline{\ \ \ \ }$

6.
$$5 = 3 + 2$$
So $5 - \underline{\ \ \ \ } = \underline{\ \ \ \ }$
and $5 - \underline{\ \ \ \ } = \underline{\ \ \ \ }$

7.
$$9 = 2 + 7$$
So $9 - \underline{\ \ \ \ } = \underline{\ \ \ \ }$
and $9 - \underline{\ \ \ \ } = \underline{\ \ \ \ }$

8.
$$4 = 3 + 1$$
So $4 - \underline{\ \ \ \ } = \underline{\ \ \ \ }$
and $4 - \underline{\ \ \ \ } = \underline{\ \ \ \ }$

$$4 = 1 + 3 \qquad 5 = 1 + 4 \qquad 6 = 1 + 5$$
$$4 = 2 + 2 \qquad 5 = 2 + 3 \qquad 6 = 2 + 4$$
$$6 = 3 + 3$$

☐ Write the addition fact you use to subtract.

9. $5 - 3$ | $5 = \underline{3} + \underline{2}$

10. $6 - 2$ | $6 = \underline{2} + \underline{}$

11. $6 - 5$ | $6 = \underline{5} + \underline{}$

12. $4 - 3$ | $4 = \underline{3} + \underline{}$

13. $6 - 3$ | $6 = \underline{} + \underline{}$

14. $6 - 4$ | $6 = \underline{} + \underline{}$

☐ Subtract by using an addition fact.

15. $6 - 4$ | $6 = \underline{4} + \underline{2}$
so $6 - 4 = \underline{2}$

16. $5 - 3$ | $5 = \underline{3} + \underline{}$
so $5 - 3 = \underline{}$

17. $6 - 3$ | $6 = \underline{} + \underline{}$
so $6 - 3 = \underline{}$

18. $4 - 3$ | $4 = \underline{} + \underline{}$
so $4 - 3 = \underline{}$

19. $5 - 2$ | $5 = \underline{} + \underline{}$
so $5 - 2 = \underline{}$

20. $6 - 5$ | $6 = \underline{} + \underline{}$
so $6 - 5 = \underline{}$

$$7 = 1 + 6 \qquad 8 = 1 + 7 \qquad 9 = 1 + 8$$
$$7 = 2 + 5 \qquad 8 = 2 + 6 \qquad 9 = 2 + 7$$
$$7 = 3 + 4 \qquad 8 = 3 + 5 \qquad 9 = 3 + 6$$
$$ \qquad 8 = 4 + 4 \qquad 9 = 4 + 5$$

☐ Subtract by using an addition fact.

21.

$7 - 2$ | $7 = \underline{\ 2\ } + \underline{\ 5\ }$
so $7 - 2 = \underline{\quad}$

22.

$7 - 3$ | $7 = \underline{\quad} + \underline{\quad}$
so $7 - 3 = \underline{\quad}$

23.

$7 - 5$ | $7 = \underline{\quad} + \underline{\quad}$
so $7 - 5 = \underline{\quad}$

24.

$7 - 4$ | $7 = \underline{\quad} + \underline{\quad}$
so $7 - 4 = \underline{\quad}$

25.

$8 - 4$ | $8 = \underline{\quad} + \underline{\quad}$
so $8 - 4 = \underline{\quad}$

26.

$8 - 3$ | $8 = \underline{\quad} + \underline{\quad}$
so $8 - 3 = \underline{\quad}$

27.

$8 - 5$ | $8 = \underline{\quad} + \underline{\quad}$
so $8 - 5 = \underline{\quad}$

28.

$9 - 4$ | $9 = \underline{\quad} + \underline{\quad}$
so $9 - 4 = \underline{\quad}$

29.

$9 - 6$ | $9 = \underline{\quad} + \underline{\quad}$
so $9 - 6 = \underline{\quad}$

30.

$9 - 7$ | $9 = \underline{\quad} + \underline{\quad}$
so $9 - 7 = \underline{\quad}$

Operations and Algebraic Thinking 1-37

$$10 = 1 + 9 \qquad \text{or} \qquad 9 + 1$$
$$10 = 2 + 8 \qquad\qquad\qquad 8 + 2$$
$$10 = 3 + 7 \qquad\qquad\qquad 7 + 3$$
$$10 = 4 + 6 \qquad\qquad\qquad 6 + 4$$
$$10 = 5 + 5 \qquad\qquad\qquad 5 + 5$$

☐ Use an addition fact to subtract.

1.
$10 - 6$ | $10 = \underline{\ 6\ } + \underline{\ 4\ }$
so $10 - 6 = \underline{\quad}$

2.
$10 - 5$ | $10 = \underline{\quad} + \underline{\quad}$
so $10 - 5 = \underline{\quad}$

3.
$10 - 7$ | $10 = \underline{\quad} + \underline{\quad}$
so $10 - 7 = \underline{\quad}$

4.
$10 - 2$ | $10 = \underline{\quad} + \underline{\quad}$
so $10 - 2 = \underline{\quad}$

5.
$10 - 4$ | $10 = \underline{\quad} + \underline{\quad}$
so $10 - 4 = \underline{\quad}$

6.
$10 - 3$ | $10 = \underline{\quad} + \underline{\quad}$
so $10 - 3 = \underline{\quad}$

☐ Subtract.

7.

$10 - 4 = \underline{\quad}$ $\qquad$ $10 - 6 = \underline{\quad}$ $\qquad$ $10 - 1 = \underline{\quad}$

$10 - 9 = \underline{\quad}$ $\qquad$ $10 - 5 = \underline{\quad}$ $\qquad$ $10 - 8 = \underline{\quad}$

$10 - 3 = \underline{\quad}$ $\qquad$ $10 - 2 = \underline{\quad}$ $\qquad$ $10 - 7 = \underline{\quad}$

☐ Write the doubles.

8.

$1 + 1 = \underline{2}$

$2 + 2 = \underline{4}$

$3 + 3 = \underline{6}$

$4 + 4 = \underline{}$

$5 + 5 = \underline{}$

$6 + 6 = \underline{12}$

$7 + 7 = \underline{14}$

$8 + 8 = \underline{}$

$9 + 9 = \underline{}$

$10 + 10 = \underline{}$

☐ Use doubles to subtract.

9.

$16 - 8$ | $\underline{8} + \underline{8} = 16$

so $16 - 8 = \underline{}$

10.

$14 - 7$ | $\underline{} + \underline{} = 14$

so $14 - 7 = \underline{}$

11.

$10 - 5$ | $\underline{} + \underline{} = 10$

so $10 - 5 = \underline{}$

12.

$6 - 3$ | $\underline{} + \underline{} = 6$

so $6 - 3 = \underline{}$

13.

$12 - 6$ | $\underline{} + \underline{} = 12$

so $12 - 6 = \underline{}$

14.

$8 - 4$ | $\underline{} + \underline{} = 8$

so $8 - 4 = \underline{}$

15.

$4 - 2$ | $\underline{} + \underline{} = 4$

so $4 - 2 = \underline{}$

16.

$20 - 10$ | $\underline{} + \underline{} = 20$

so $20 - 10 = \underline{}$

Operations and Algebraic Thinking 1-38

OAI-39 Subtract to Get 10

☐ Use a chart to subtract.

1.

1	2	3	4	5	6	7	8	9	10

☒	☒	☒

$13 - 3 = \underline{\ 10\ }$

2.

1	2	3	4	5	6	7	8	9	10

11	12	13	14	15

$15 - 5 = \underline{\quad\quad}$

3.

1	2	3	4	5	6	7	8	9	10

11	12	13	14

$14 - 4 = \underline{\quad\quad}$

4.

1	2	3	4	5	6	7	8	9	10

11	12	13	14	15	16

$16 - 6 = \underline{\quad\quad}$

5.

1	2	3	4	5	6	7	8	9	10

11	12	13	14	15	16	17	18	19

$19 - 9 = \underline{\quad\quad}$

6.

1	2	3	4	5	6	7	8	9	10

11	12	13	14	15	16	17

$17 - 7 = \underline{\quad\quad}$

☐ Subtract.

7.
13 − 3 = _____

8.
17 − 7 = _____

9.
18 − 8 = _____

10.
12 − 2 = _____

11.
15 − 5 = _____

12.
16 − 6 = _____

13.
19 − 9 = _____

14.
14 − 4 = _____

15.
11 − 1 = _____

☐ Fill in the blank.

16.
17 − _____ = 10

17.
18 − _____ = 10

18.
11 − _____ = 10

19.
12 − _____ = 10

20.
13 − _____ = 10

21.
19 − _____ = 10

22.
15 − _____ = 10

23.
14 − _____ = 10

24.
16 − _____ = 10

☐ Find the answer.

25.

Grace has 12 apples.

She eats 2 of them.

How many are left?

Operations and Algebraic Thinking 1-39

OAI-40 Subtracting from the Teens Using 10

⬜ Take away 🔲 to get to 10.
⬜ Then take away ⬜ from 10.

1.

15 − 7

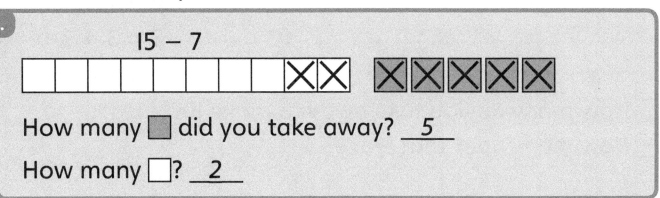

How many 🔲 did you take away? __5__

How many ⬜? __2__

2.

14 − 6

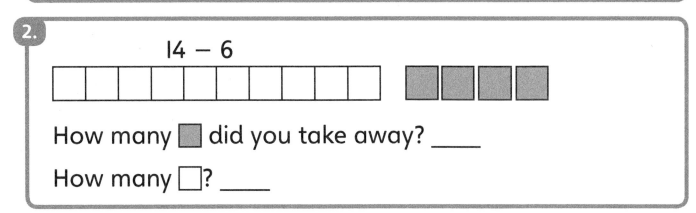

How many 🔲 did you take away? ____

How many ⬜? ____

3.

16 − 8

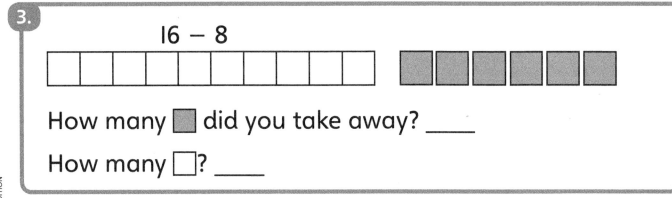

How many 🔲 did you take away? ____

How many ⬜? ____

4.

13 − 7

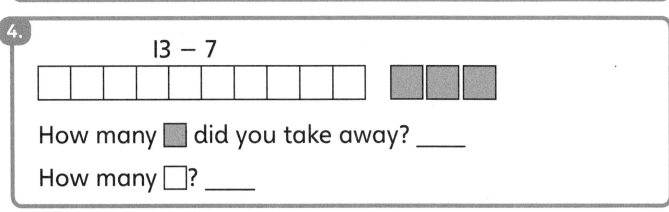

How many 🔲 did you take away? ____

How many ⬜? ____

$$4 = 1 + 3 \qquad 5 = 1 + 4 \qquad 6 = 1 + 5$$
$$4 = 2 + 2 \qquad 5 = 2 + 3 \qquad 6 = 2 + 4$$
$$6 = 3 + 3$$

☐ How many do you take away to make 10?
☐ How many does that leave?

5.

$$12 \quad - \quad 6$$

$$12 - \underline{\ \ 2\ \ } - \underline{\ \ 4\ \ }$$

This makes 10.

6.

$$14 \quad - \quad 6$$

$$14 - \underline{\ \ 4\ \ } - \underline{\ \ \ \ }$$

This makes 10.

7.

$$12 \quad - \quad 5$$

$$12 - \underline{\ \ 2\ \ } - \underline{\ \ \ \ }$$

8.

$$14 \quad - \quad 5$$

$$14 - \underline{\ \ 4\ \ } - \underline{\ \ \ \ }$$

9.

$$13 \quad - \quad 4$$

$$13 - \underline{\ \ 3\ \ } - \underline{\ \ \ \ }$$

10.

$$12 \quad - \quad 4$$

$$12 - \underline{\ \ \ \ } - \underline{\ \ \ \ }$$

11.

$$15 \quad - \quad 6$$

$$15 - \underline{\ \ \ \ } - \underline{\ \ \ \ }$$

12.

$$11 \quad - \quad 6$$

$$11 - \underline{\ \ \ \ } - \underline{\ \ \ \ }$$

$$7 = 1 + 6 \qquad 8 = 1 + 7 \qquad 9 = 1 + 8$$

$$7 = 2 + 5 \qquad 8 = 2 + 6 \qquad 9 = 2 + 7$$

$$7 = 3 + 4 \qquad 8 = 3 + 5 \qquad 9 = 3 + 6$$

$$8 = 4 + 4 \qquad 9 = 4 + 5$$

☐ How many do you take away to make 10?
☐ How many does that leave?

13.

16   −   7

16 − __6__ − __1__

14.

12   −   8

12 − __2__ − ____

15.

15   −   8

15 − ____ − ____

16.

14   −   7

14 − ____ − ____

17.

15   −   9

15 − ____ − ____

18.

16   −   8

16 − ____ − ____

19.

17   −   9

17 − ____ − ____

20.

11   −   7

11 − ____ − ____

☐ Subtract by making 10.

21.

13   −   5

= 13 − __3__ − __2__

= 10 − __2__

= __8__

22.

15   −   8

= 15 − __5__ − ____

= 10 − ____

= ____

23.

16   −   7

= 16 − ____ − ____

= 10 − ____

= ____

24.

12   −   6

= 12 − ____ − ____

= 10 − ____

= ____

25.

15   −   7

= 15 − ____ − ____

= 10 − ____

= ____

26.

14   −   5

= 14 − ____ − ____

= 10 − ____

= ____

27.   13 − 8

28.   14 − 7

29.   18 − 9

30.   17 − 8

31.   13 − 4

32.   15 − 6

33.   16 − 9

34.   12 − 4

Operations and Algebraic Thinking 1-40

OAI-41 Subtraction Word Problems

☐ Draw a picture to subtract.

1.

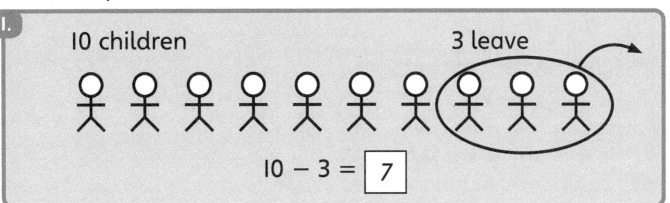

10 children   3 leave

10 − 3 = [7]

2.

8 children   5 leave

8 − 5 = ☐

3.

6 children   2 leave

6 − 2 = ☐

4.

7 children   5 leave

7 − 5 = ☐

☐ Draw circles to subtract.

5.

10 flies are buzzing.

A frog eats 4 of them.

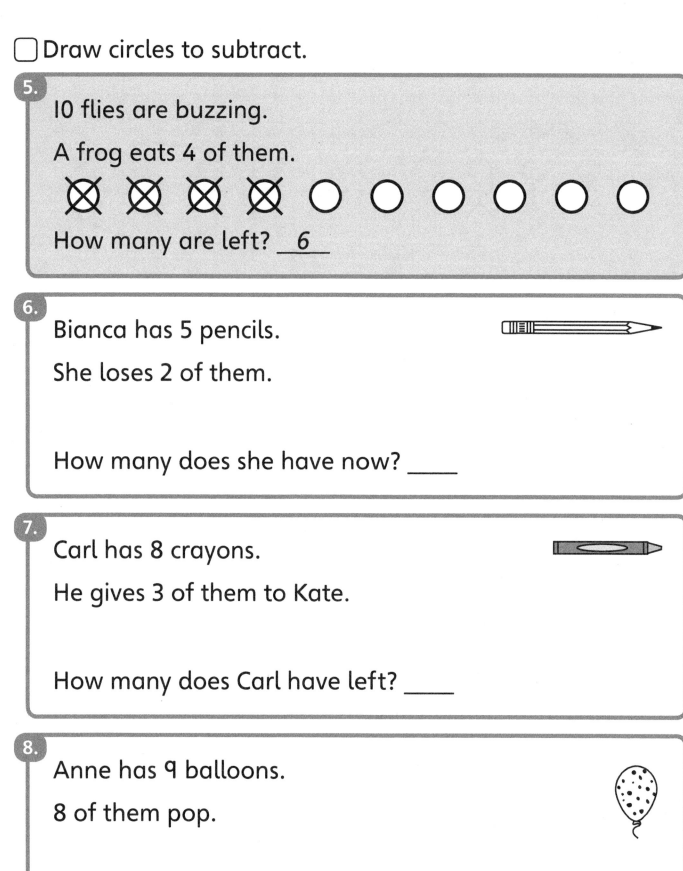

How many are left? __6__

6.

Bianca has 5 pencils.

She loses 2 of them.

How many does she have now? ____

7.

Carl has 8 crayons.

He gives 3 of them to Kate.

How many does Carl have left? ____

8.

Anne has 9 balloons.

8 of them pop.

How many are left? ____

Operations and Algebraic Thinking 1-41

Draw circles to subtract.

9.

8 children play soccer.

4 leave to go down a slide.

How many are still playing soccer? _____

10.

5 birds are on a tree.

3 of them fly away.

How many birds are on the tree now? _____

11.

Roy has 8 stamps.

He uses 3 of them.

How many stamps are left? _____

12.

6 puppies are in a box.

2 climb out.

How many are in the box now? _____

MDI-I Length

☐ Color the **longer** pencil.

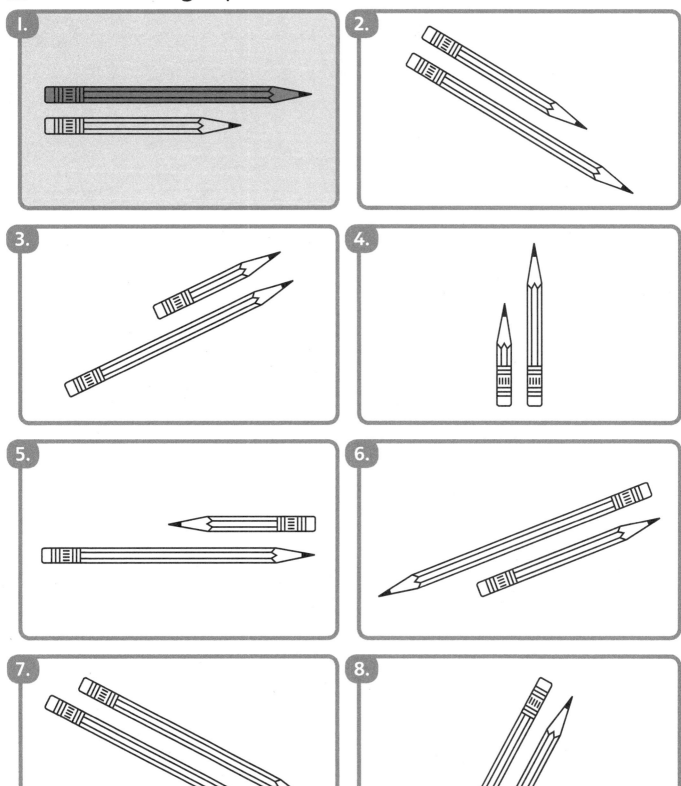

1.

2.

3.

4.

5.

6.

7.

8.

☐ Color the **longer** pencil.

9.
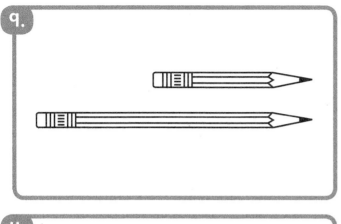

10.
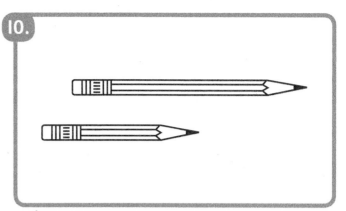

11.
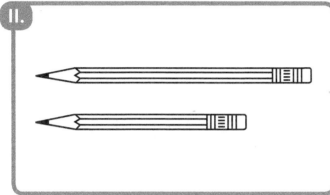

12.
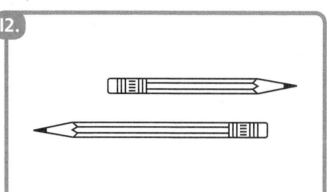

☐ Color the **shorter** pencil.

13.
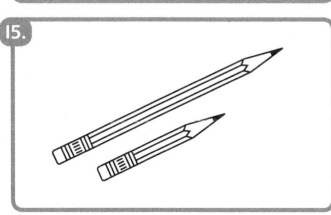

14.
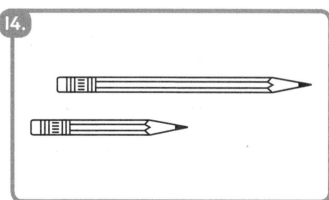

15.
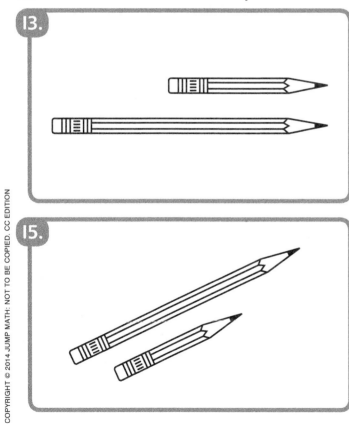

16. BONUS
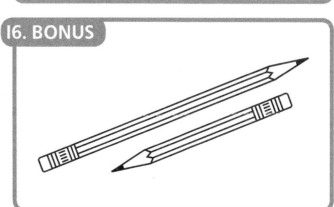

☐ Draw the object.

17.

a **shorter** pencil

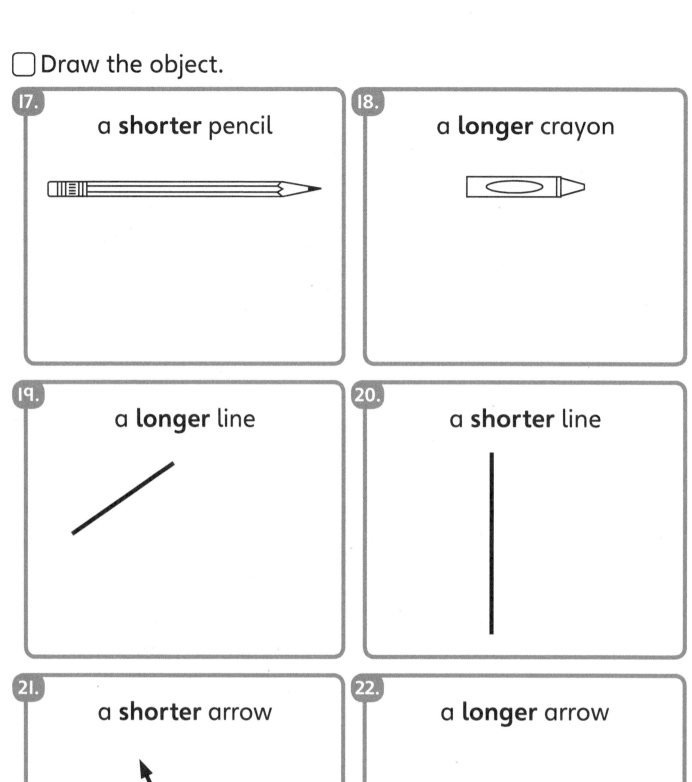

18.

a **longer** crayon

19.

a **longer** line

20.

a **shorter** line

21.

a **shorter** arrow

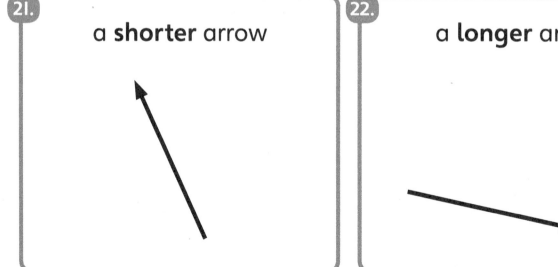

22.

a **longer** arrow

MDI-2 Width

☐ Circle the answer.

1.

Which is **wider**?

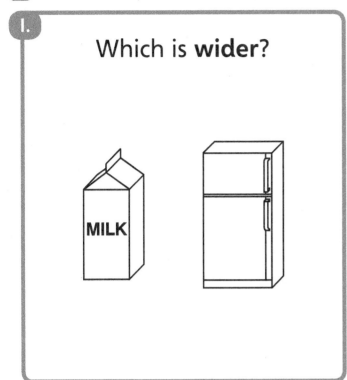

2.

Which is **narrower**?

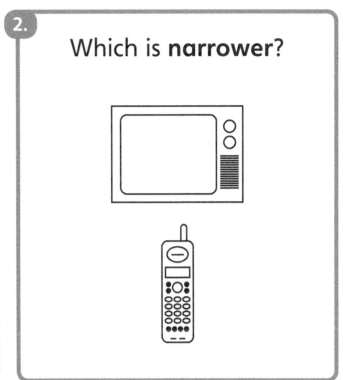

3.

Which is **widest**?

4.

Which is **narrowest**?

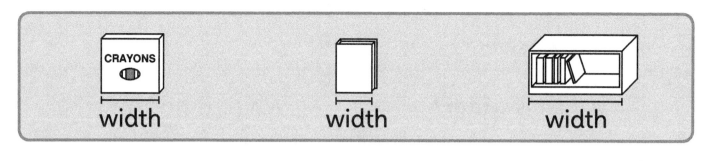

width   width   width

☐ Color the line showing the **width**.

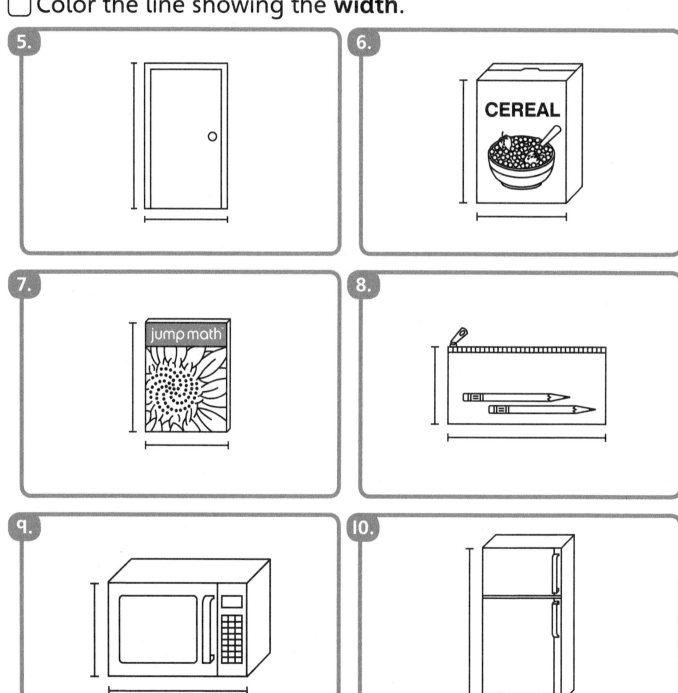

5.

6.

CEREAL

7.

jump math

8.

9.

10.

☐ Draw the object.

11.

a **wider** window

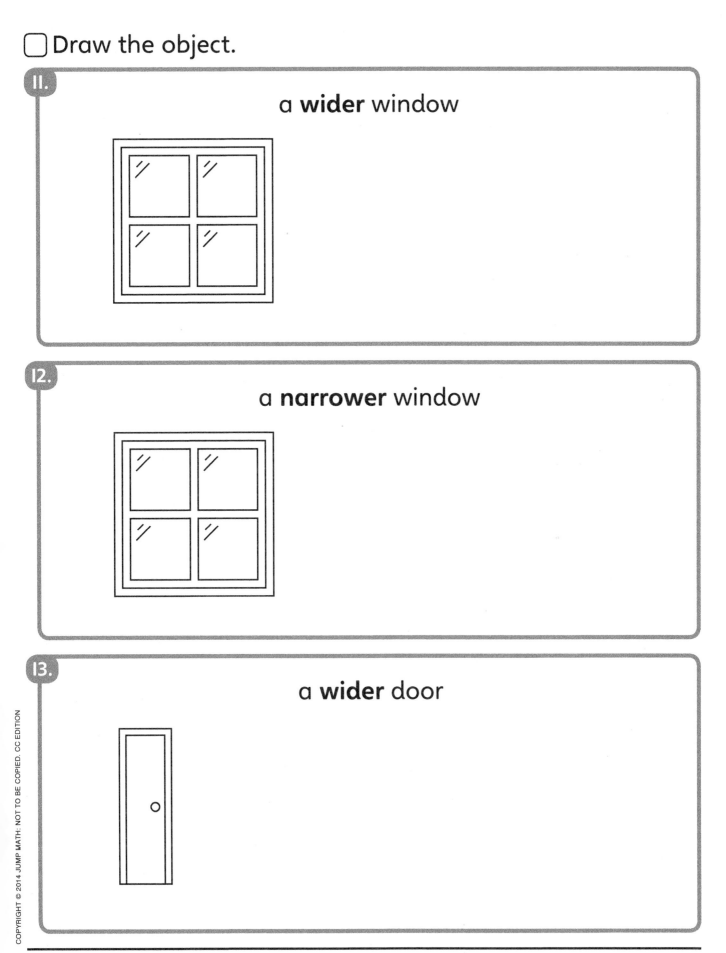

12.

a **narrower** window

13.

a **wider** door

MDI-3 Height

☐ Circle the answer.

1.

Who is **shorter**?

2.

Who is **shortest**?

3.

Which is **taller**?

4.

Which is **tallest**?

☐ Draw the object.

5.

a **shorter** sign

6.

a **taller** candle

☐ Write **taller** or **shorter**.

7.

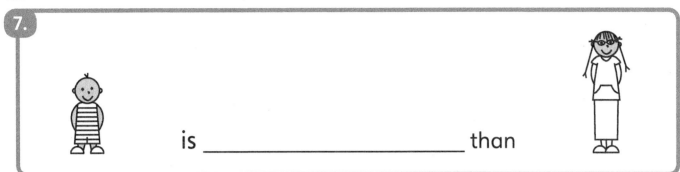

is _____ than

8.

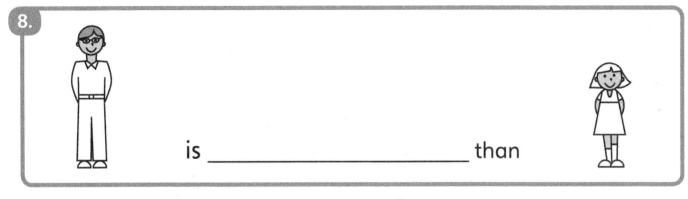

is _____ than

9.

is _____ than

☐ Circle the **tallest** person.

10.

11.

☐ Write **taller** or **wider**.

12.

is _____ than

13.

is _____ than

14.

Chicken Soup

is _____ than

SODA

15.

SODA

is _____ than

Chicken Soup

16.

is _____ than

17.

is _____ than

MDI-4 Comparing Lengths

☐ Draw 3 lines with different lengths.
☐ Start at the dots.

1.

shortest •————————

in between •————————————

longest •————————————————————

2.

longest •

in between •

shortest •

3.

shortest •

longest •

in between •

4.

in between •

longest •

shortest •

☐ Draw 3 pencils with different lengths.
☐ Start at the dots.

5.

shortest   ●

longest   ●

in between   ●

6.

longest   ●

in between   ●

shortest   ●

7.

longest   ●

shortest   ●

in between   ●

8.

shortest   ●

in between   ●

longest   ●

Measurement and Data 1-4

☐ Draw a crayon that is shorter than the pencil.
☐ Draw a line that is longer than the pencil.

9.

crayon ●

pencil

line ●

Which is longer, the crayon or the line?

_____

☐ Draw a crayon that is longer than the pencil.
☐ Draw a line that is shorter than the pencil.

10.

crayon ●

pencil

line ●

Which is longer, the crayon or the line?

_____

11. Draw 4 objects from longest to shortest.

☐ Circle the answer.

12.

⬛➤ is shorter than ✏️

🖌️ is longer than ✏️

Which is longer? ⬛➤   🖌️

13.

⬛➤ is longer than ✏️

🖌️ is shorter than ✏️

Which is longer? ⬛➤   🖌️

14.

⬛ is longer than ✏️

⬛➤ is shorter than ✏️

Which is longer? ⬛   ⬛➤

15. BONUS

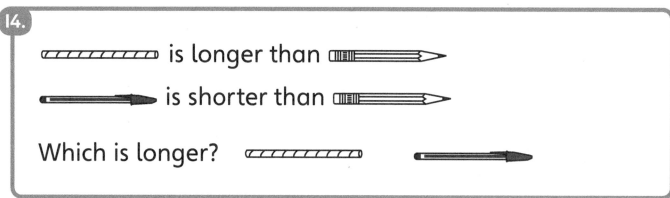

⬛➤ is longer than ✏️

✏️ is longer than 🖌️

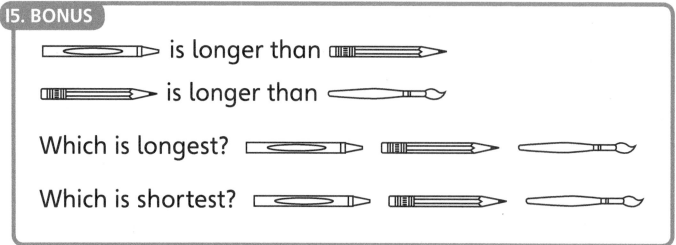

Which is longest? ⬛➤ ✏️ 🖌️

Which is shortest? ⬛➤ ✏️ 🖌️

MDI-5 More Comparing Lengths

☐ Can you straighten the object to make it **longer**?

1.

_no_

2.

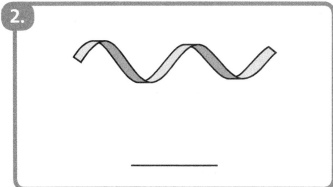

_____

3.

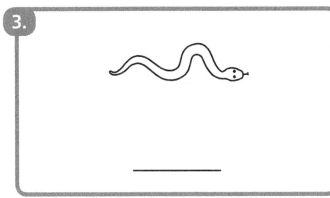

_____

4.

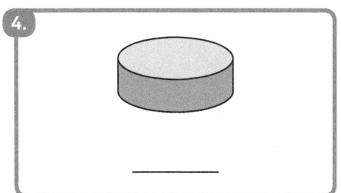

_____

☐ Circle the **longer** object.

5.

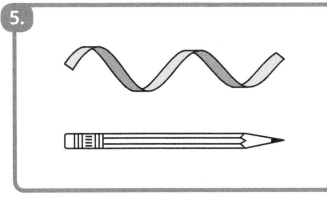

6.

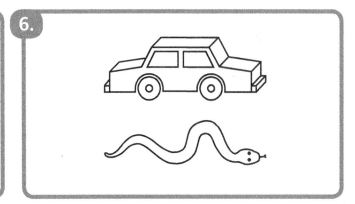

7.

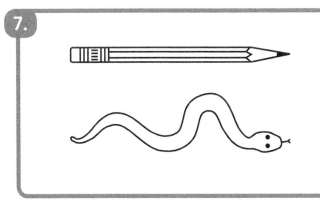

8.

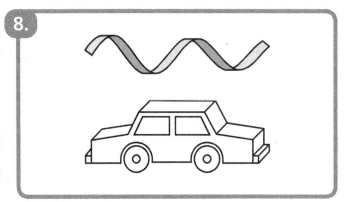

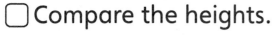 Compare the heights.
☐ Where does the pencil fit?

9.

1 2 3

is between ___ and ___.

10.

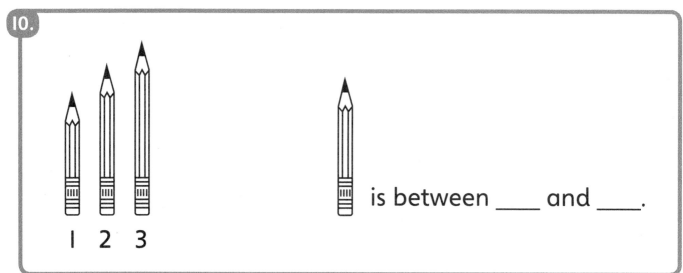

1 2 3

is between ___ and ___.

11.

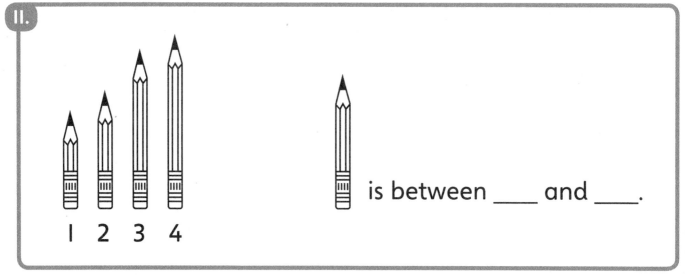

1 2 3 4

is between ___ and ___.

Measurement and Data I-5

☐ Draw the object.

1. Something **taller** than a meter stick is long.

2. Something **longer** than a meter stick is long.

3. Something **wider** than a meter stick is long.

☐ How many meter sticks long?

4.

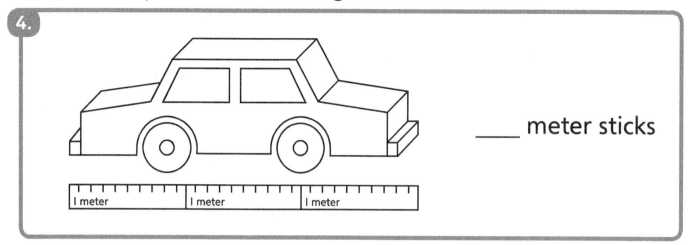

____ meter sticks

5.

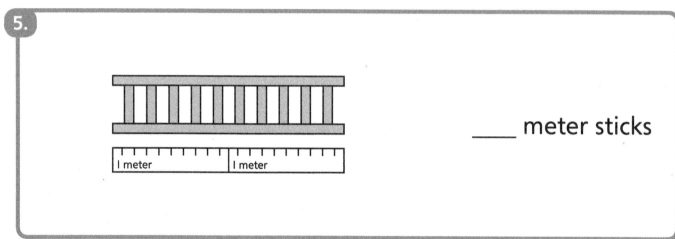

____ meter sticks

☐ Circle the answer.

6.

A table is longer than a meter stick.

A desk is shorter than a meter stick.

Which is longer?   table   desk

7.

A fish is shorter than a meter stick.

A dog is longer than a meter stick.

Which is longer?   fish   dog

MDI-7 Length (Advanced)

☐ Make 4 strips of paper. Use them to compare.

☐ Is the top of the picture **longer** or **shorter** than its side?

1.

shorter

2.

_____

3.

_____

4.

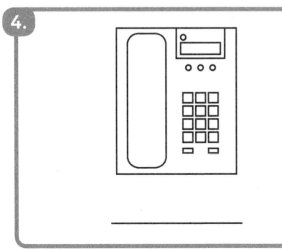

_____

5.

_____

Which is longer?
☐ Measure with a strip of paper.
☐ Write **A**, **B**, or **same**.

6.

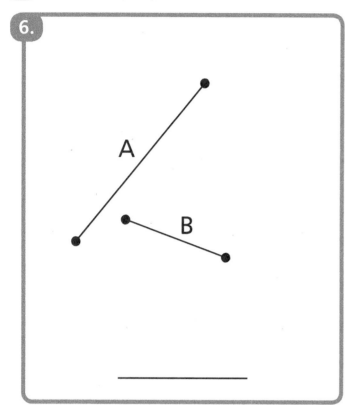

_____

7.

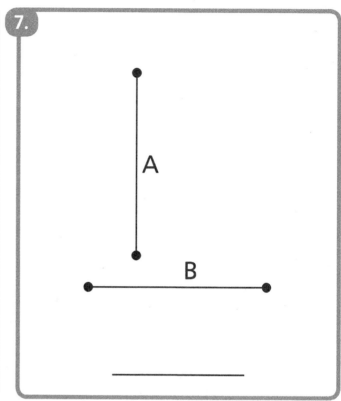

_____

8.

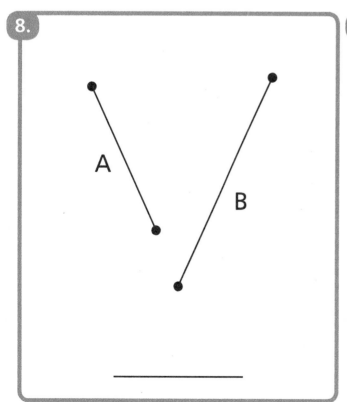

_____

9. BONUS

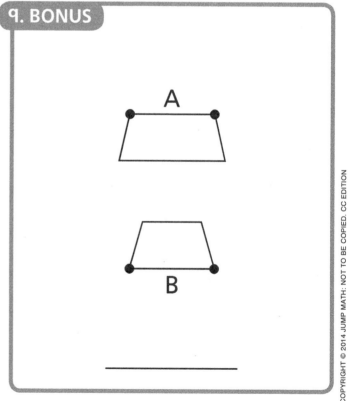

_____

Measurement and Data 1-7

MDI-8 Measuring Length

☐ Measure each pencil.
☐ Color the **longer** pencil and circle the **larger** number.

1.
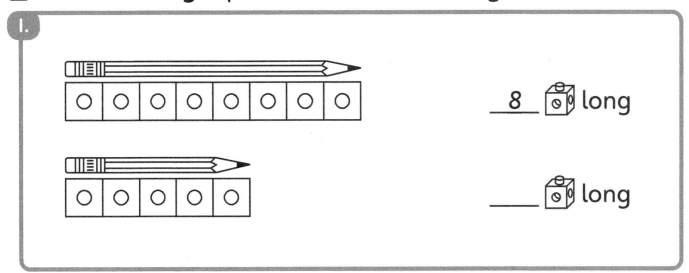

___8___ 🧊 long

_____ 🧊 long

2.
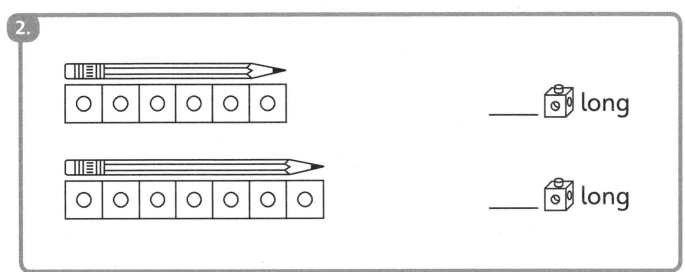

_____ 🧊 long

_____ 🧊 long

3.
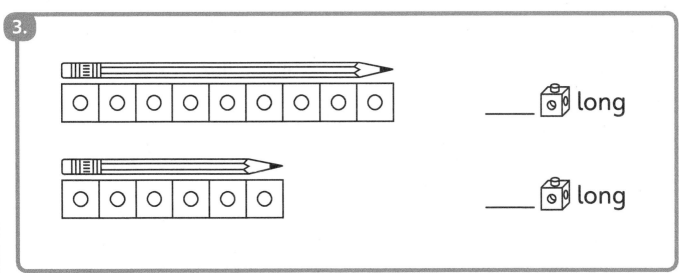

_____ 🧊 long

_____ 🧊 long

☐ Measure each pencil.
☐ Color the **longer** pencil and circle the **larger** number.

4.

_____ 🎲 long

_____ 🎲 long

☐ Whose pencil is **longer?**

5.

Will   10 🎲 long

(Rani)   13 🎲 long

6.

Nina   11 🎲 long

Carl   9 🎲 long

7.

Helen   17 🎲 long

Ivan   16 🎲 long

8.

Mike   6 🎲 long

Amy   8 🎲 long

9.

Beth   5 🎲 long

Marco   13 🎲 long

10.

Tony   14 🎲 long

Lily   10 🎲 long

MDI-9 Measuring Distance

☐ How far does the ant walk to school?

1.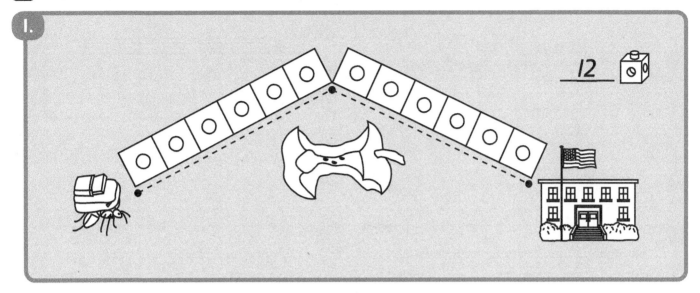

_12_

2.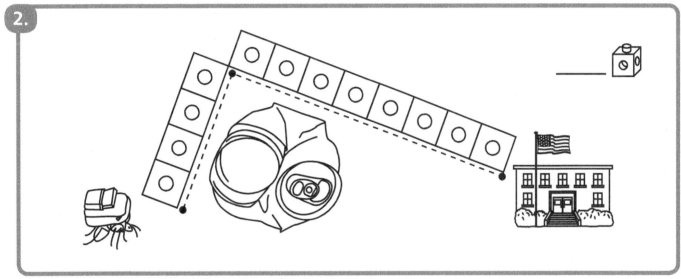

3.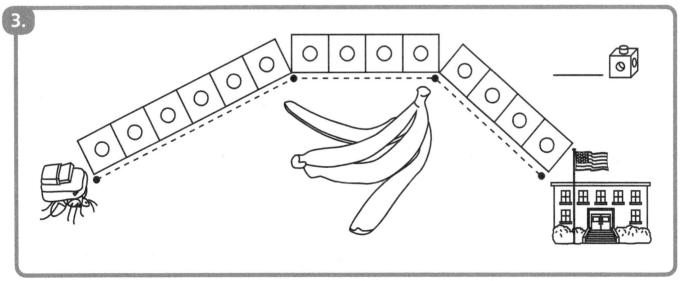

MDI-10 Units of Measurement

☐ Mark the answer as right ✓ or wrong ✗.

1.

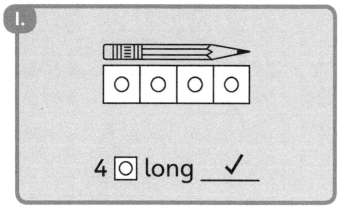

4 ◎ long ____ ✓

2.

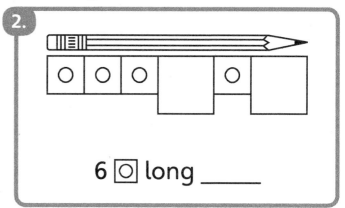

6 ◎ long ____

3.

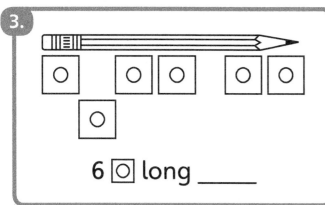

6 ◎ long ____

4.

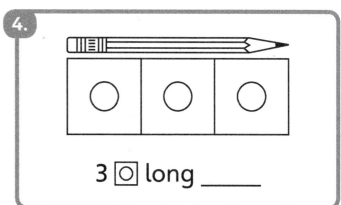

3 ◎ long ____

5.

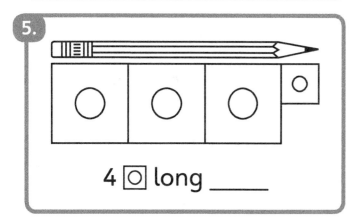

4 ◎ long ____

6.

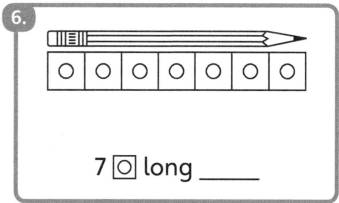

7 ◎ long ____

7.

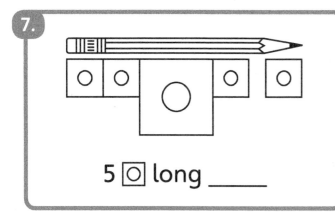

5 ◎ long ____

8.

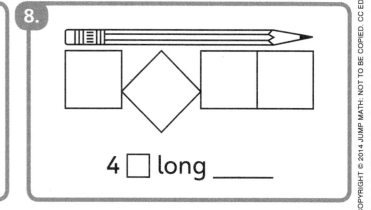

4 ☐ long ____

MDI-II Measuring Using a Ruler

◻ How many **blocks** long is the pencil?

1.

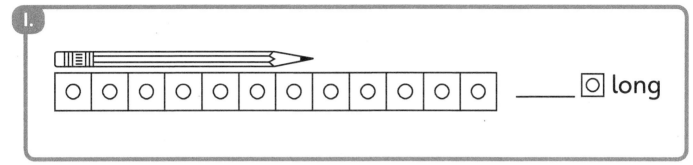

_____ ◙ long

2.

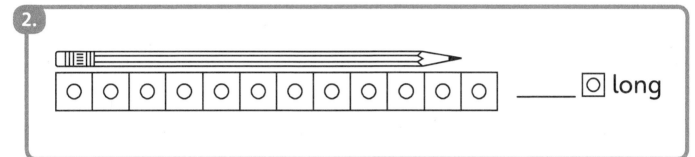

_____ ◙ long

3.

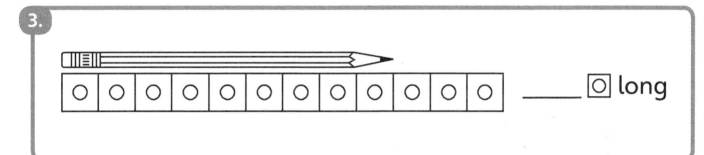

_____ ◙ long

4.

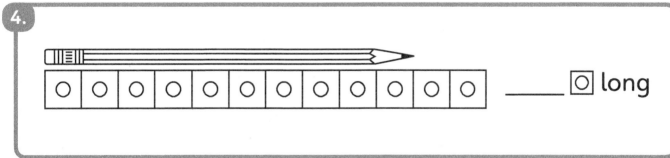

_____ ◙ long

5. BONUS

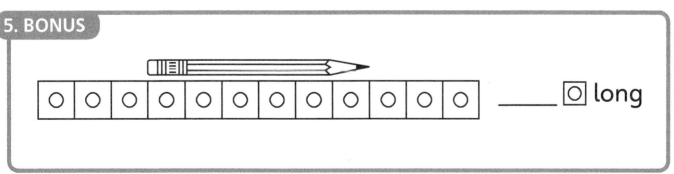

_____ ◙ long

A ruler counts the blocks for you.

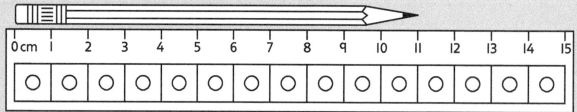

The pencil is 11 ◙ long.

☐ How many ◙ long?

6.

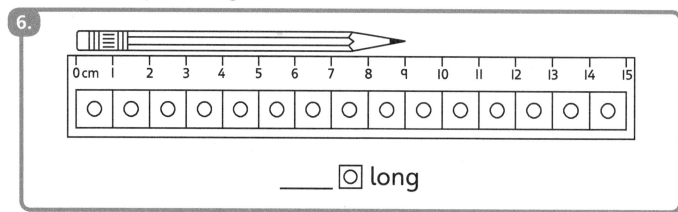

_____ ◙ long

7.

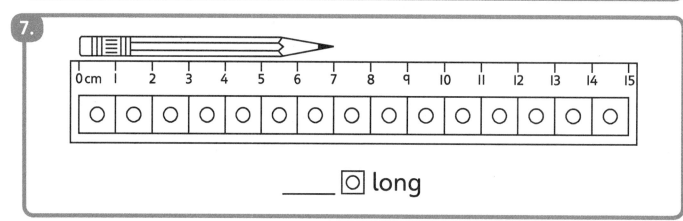

_____ ◙ long

8.

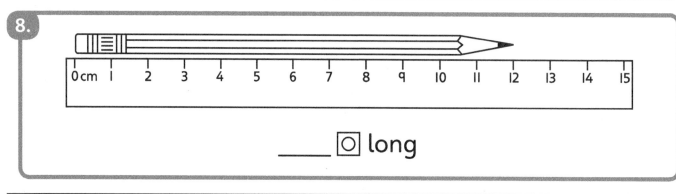

_____ ◙ long

Measurement and Data 1-11

 How many ◎ long?

9.

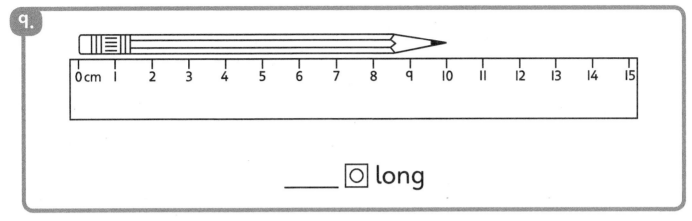

_____ ◎ long

10.

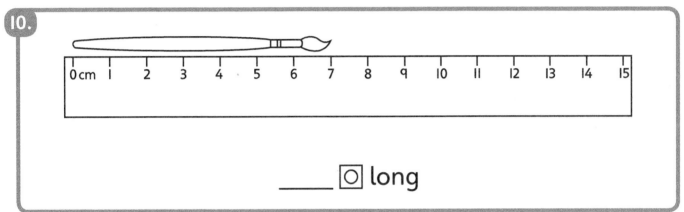

_____ ◎ long

11.

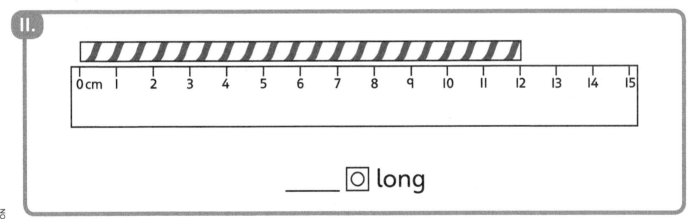

_____ ◎ long

12.

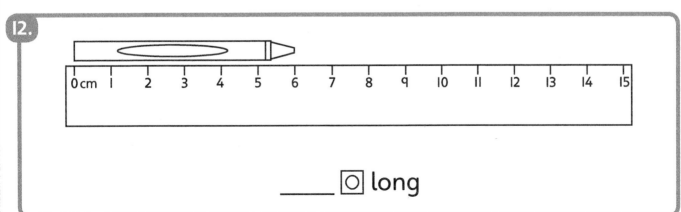

_____ ◎ long

MDI-I2 Measuring with Two Units

☐ How long is the pencil?

I.

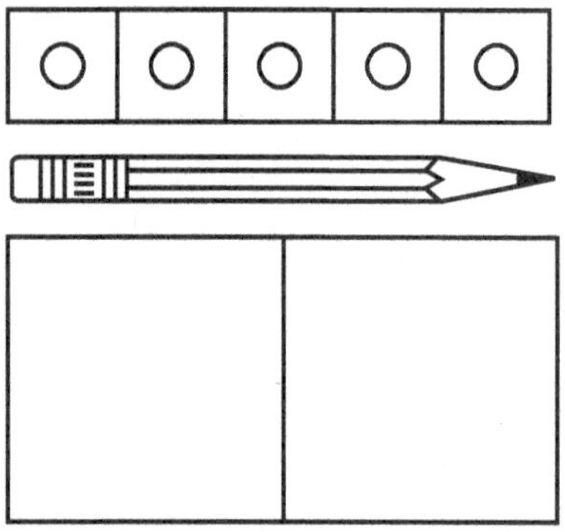

_____ 🔘 long

_____ ☐ long

2.

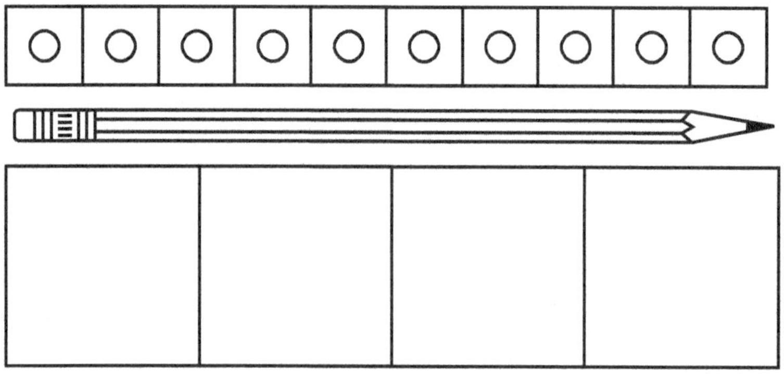

_____ 🔘 long

_____ ☐ long

3. BONUS

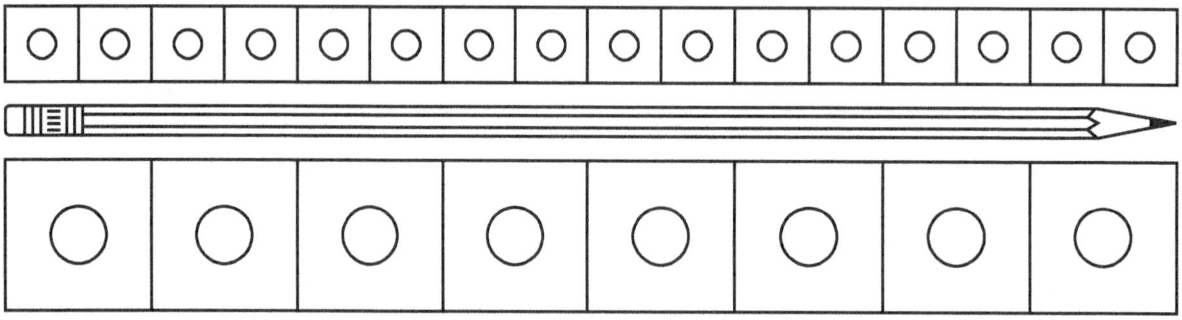

_____ 🔘 long   _____ ◯ long

connecting cube

pattern block square

☐ Measure the object.

4.

_____ ◙ long   _____ ☐ long

5.

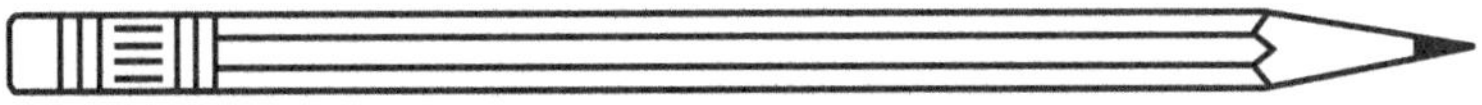

_____ ◙ long   _____ ☐ long

6.

_____ ◙ long   _____ ☐ long

◻ Measure the object.

7.

Glue

_____ ◉ long   _____ ◻ long

8.

_____ ◉ long   _____ ◻ long

q.

_____ ◉ long   _____ ◻ long

I0.

_____ ◉ long   _____ ◻ long

OAI-42 Making I0 to Add

☐ Use the group of I0 to help you add.

1.

7   5

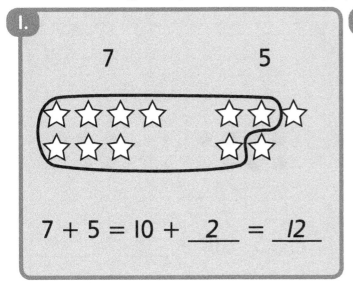

7 + 5 = I0 + __2__ = __I2__

2.

7   6

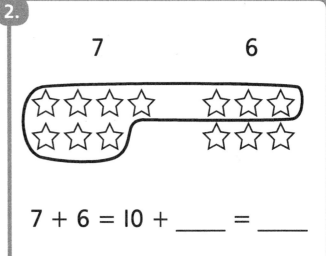

7 + 6 = I0 + ____ = ____

3.

q   5

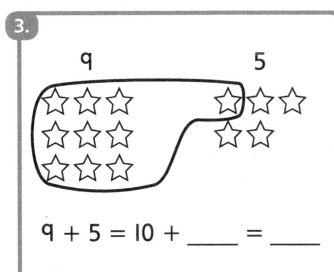

q + 5 = I0 + ____ = ____

4.

6   8

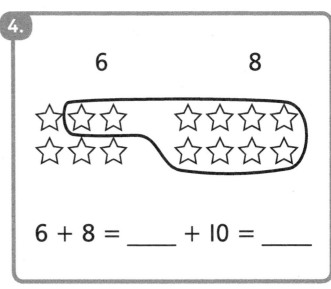

6 + 8 = ____ + I0 = ____

5.

4   8

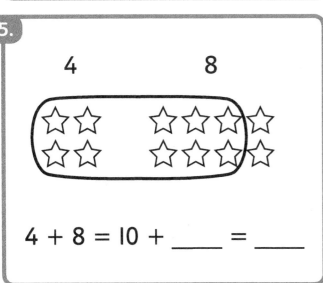

4 + 8 = I0 + ____ = ____

6.

3   q

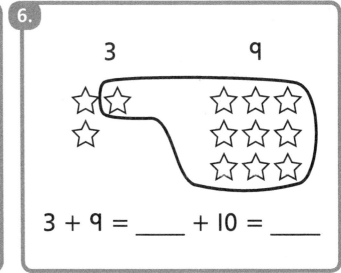

3 + q = ____ + I0 = ____

Circle a group of 10 dots.

Use 10 to add.

7.

5   8

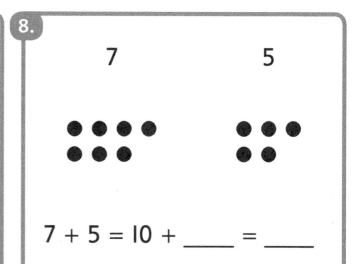

$5 + 8 = 10 + \underline{\ 3\ } = \underline{\ 13\ }$

8.

7   5

$7 + 5 = 10 + \underline{\ \ \ \ } = \underline{\ \ \ \ }$

9.

9   3

$9 + 3 = \underline{\ \ \ \ } + 10 = \underline{\ \ \ \ }$

10.

8   4

$8 + 4 = 10 + \underline{\ \ \ \ } = \underline{\ \ \ \ }$

11.

6   7

$6 + 7 = 10 + \underline{\ \ \ \ } = \underline{\ \ \ \ }$

12.

3   8

$3 + 8 = \underline{\ \ \ \ } + 10 = \underline{\ \ \ \ }$

Operations and Algebraic Thinking 1-42

OAI-43 Addition Greater Than 10

☐ Underline the blocks needed to make 10.
☐ Write the number.

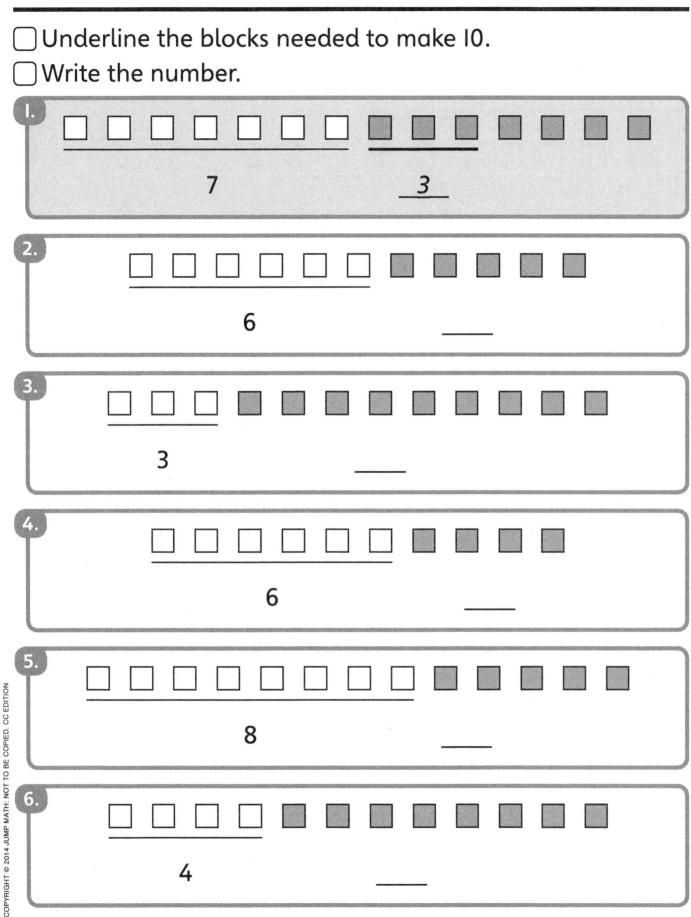

1.   7   *3*

2.   6   ____

3.   3   ____

4.   6   ____

5.   8   ____

6.   4   ____

◻ Underline the blocks needed to make 10.
◻ Circle the rest.
◻ Write the numbers.

7.

◻ ◻ ◻ ◻ ▣ ▣ ▣ ▣ ▣ ▣ (▣ ▣)

4   _6_   _2_

8.

◻ ◻ ◻ ◻ ◻ ▣ ▣ ▣ ▣ ▣ ▣ ▣ ▣

5   ___   ___

9.

◻ ◻ ◻ ◻ ◻ ◻ ◻ ◻ ▣ ▣ ▣ ▣ ▣

8   ___   ___

10.

◻ ◻ ◻ ◻ ◻ ◻ ◻ ▣ ▣ ▣ ▣ ▣ ▣ ▣ ▣

7   ___   ___

11.

◻ ◻ ◻ ◻ ◻ ◻ ◻ ◻ ▣ ▣ ▣ ▣ ▣ ▣ ▣

8   ___   ___

           Operations and Algebraic Thinking 1-43

☐How many blocks do you add to make 10?

☐How many are left?

☐Use 10 to add.

12.

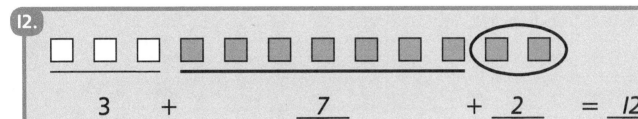

3   +   _7_   + _2_ = _12_

13.

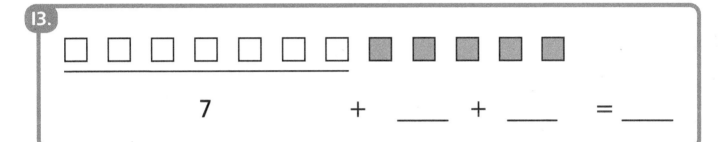

7   + ___ + ___ = ___

14.

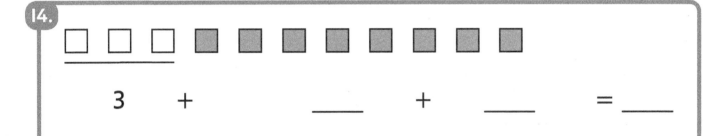

3   +   ___   +   ___   = ___

15.

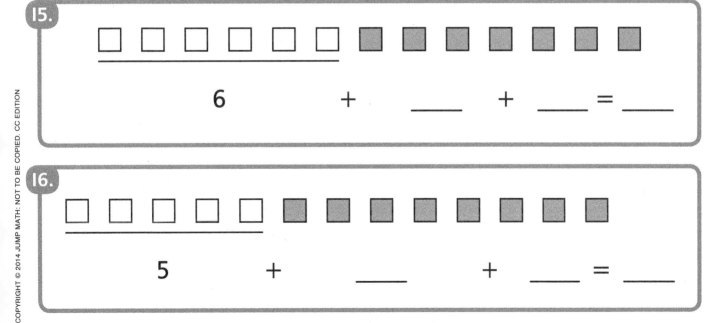

6   + ___ + ___ = ___

16.

5   +   ___   + ___ = ___

Operations and Algebraic Thinking 1-43

OAI-44 More Addition Greater Than 10

☐ Add the white blocks and the gray blocks.
☐ Count all the blocks.

1.

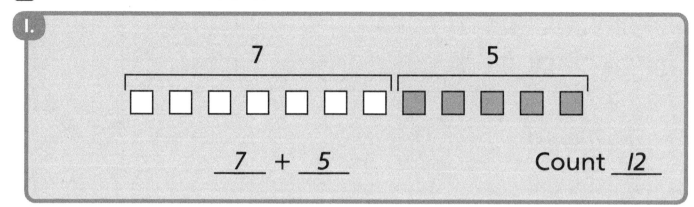

7   5

_7_ + _5_   Count _12_

2.

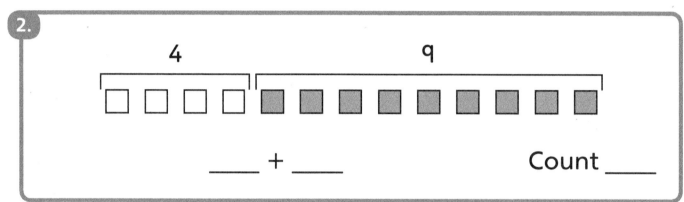

4   q

___ + ___   Count ___

3.

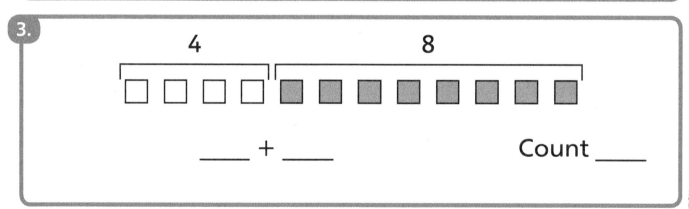

4   8

___ + ___   Count ___

4.

8   6

___ + ___   Count ___

☐ Underline the blocks needed to make 10.

☐ Circle the rest.

☐ Add.

5.

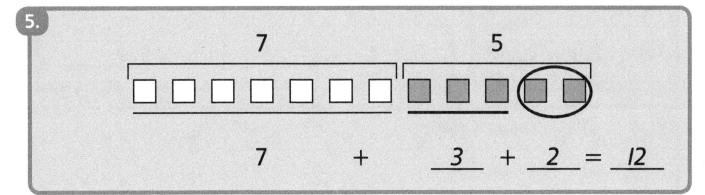

7   5

7   +   _3_ + _2_ = _12_

6.

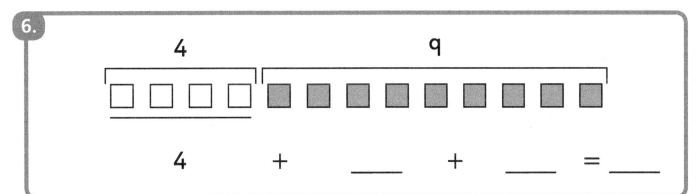

4   q

4   +   ___ + ___ = ___

7.

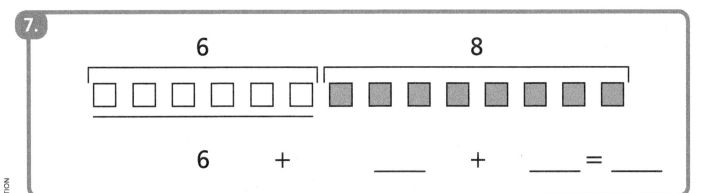

6   8

6   +   ___ + ___ = ___

8.

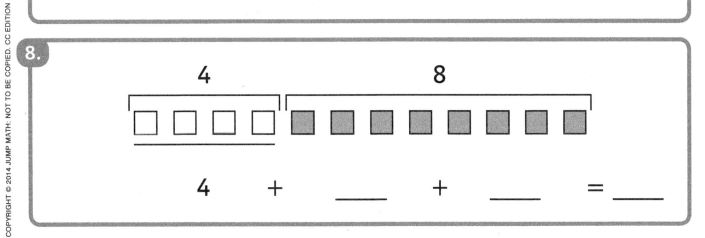

4   8

4   +   ___ + ___ = ___

☐ When you add to make 10, how many are left?

9.
8 + 5

8 + 2 + _3_

10.
6 + 8

6 + 4 + ____

11.
5 + 9

5 + 5 + ____

12.
2 + 9

2 + 8 + ____

13.
4 + 8

4 + 6 + ____

14.
3 + 9

3 + 7 + ____

15.
8 + 9

8 + 2 + ____

16.
7 + 6

7 + 3 + ____

17.
3 + 8

3 + 7 + ____

☐ Fill in the blank.

18.
5 + 7

5 + 5 + ____

19.
6 + 7

6 + 4 + ____

20.
8 + 4

8 + 2 + ____

21.
9 + 3

9 + 1 + ____

22.
2 + 9

2 + 8 + ____

23.
4 + 7

4 + 6 + ____

Operations and Algebraic Thinking 1-44

☐ How many do you add to make 10?
☐ How many are left?

24.
8   +   3

8 + ___ + ___

25.
5   +   6

5 + ___ + ___

26.
8   +   5

8 + ___ + ___

27.
6   +   6

6 + ___ + ___

28.
3   +   9

3 + ___ + ___

29.
7   +   7

7 + ___ + ___

☐ Add using 10.

30.
7   +   9

= 7 + ___ + ___

= 10 + ___

= ___

31.
6   +   5

= 6 + ___ + ___

= 10 + ___

= ___

32.
3   +   9

= 3 + ___ + ___

= 10 + ___

= ___

33.
8   +   4

= 8 + ___ + ___

= 10 + ___

= ___

34.
6   +   9

= 6 + ___ + ___

= 10 + ___

= ___

35.
5   +   8

= 5 + ___ + ___

= 10 + ___

= ___

OAI-45 Comparing to 5

☐ Count the fingers that are up.
☐ How many more than 5?

1.

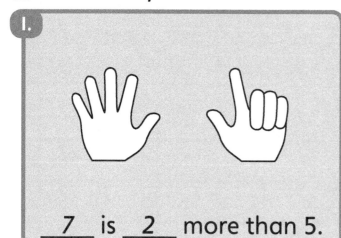

_7_ is _2_ more than 5.

2.

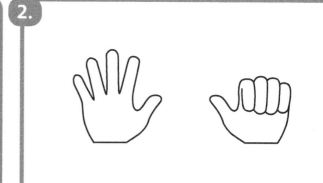

_6_ is ___ more than 5.

3.

___ is ___ more than 5.

4.

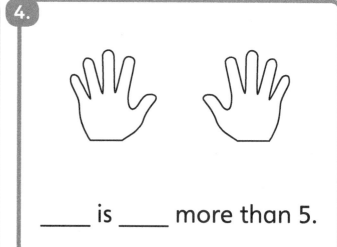

___ is ___ more than 5.

5.

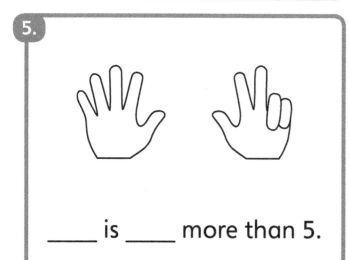

___ is ___ more than 5.

6.

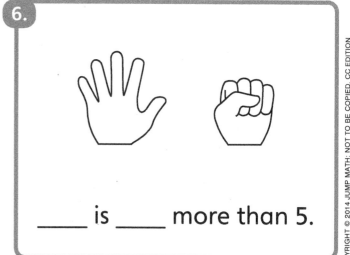

___ is ___ more than 5.

 Count the fingers that are **not** up.
How many less than 5?

7.

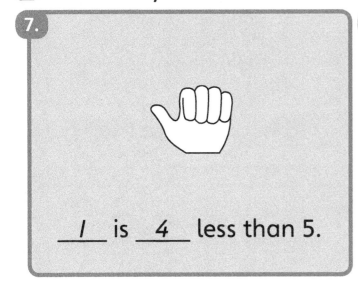

___/___ is ___4___ less than 5.

8.

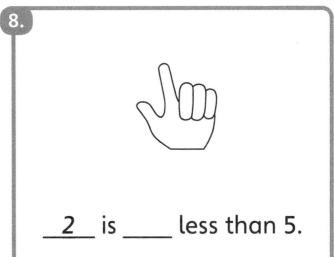

___2___ is _____ less than 5.

9.

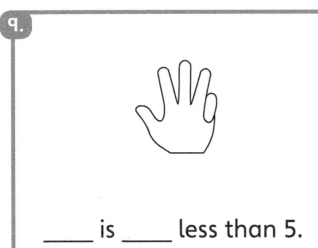

_____ is _____ less than 5.

10.

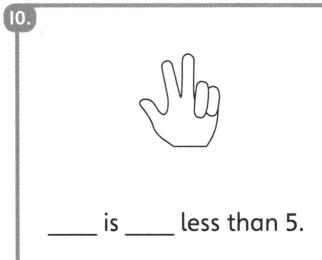

_____ is _____ less than 5.

11.

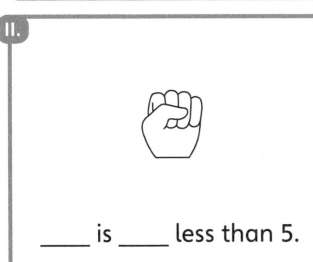

_____ is _____ less than 5.

12.

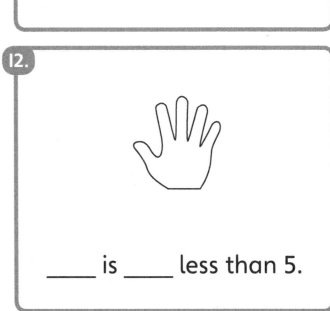

_____ is _____ less than 5.

How many more than 5?

13.

7 is __2__ more than 5.

14.

8 is ____ more than 5.

15.

6 is ____ more than 5.

16.

9 is ____ more than 5.

How many less than 5?

17.

2 is ____ less than 5.

18.

1 is ____ less than 5.

19.

3 is ____ less than 5.

20.

4 is ____ less than 5.

Operations and Algebraic Thinking 1-45

How many more or less than 5?

21.

____ is ____ more than 5.

22.

____ is ____ less than 5.

23.

____ is ____ more than 5.

24.

____ is ____ more than 5.

25.

____ is ____ less than 5.

26.

____ is ____ less than 5.

27.

____ is ____ less than 5.

28.

____ is ____ more than 5.

☐ Draw the number of dots.
☐ Fill in the blank.

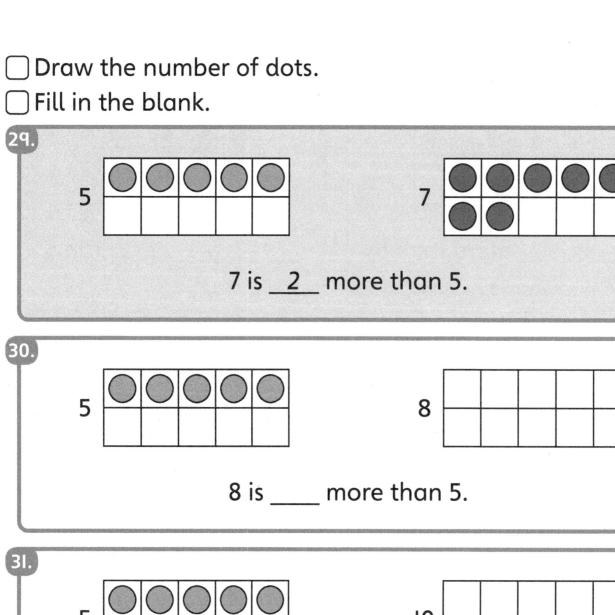

29.

5 ⬤⬤⬤⬤⬤

7 ⬤⬤⬤⬤⬤
   ⬤⬤

7 is __2__ more than 5.

30.

5 ⬤⬤⬤⬤⬤

8

8 is _____ more than 5.

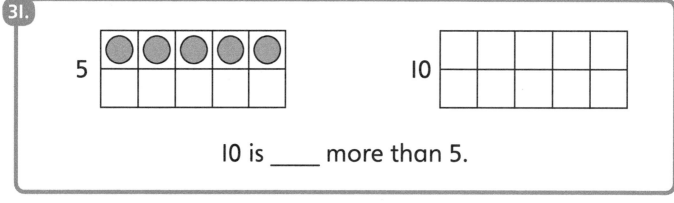

31.

5 ⬤⬤⬤⬤⬤

10

10 is _____ more than 5.

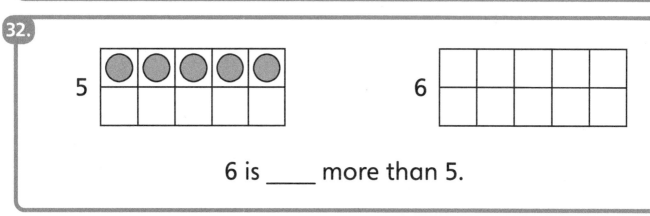

32.

5 ⬤⬤⬤⬤⬤

6

6 is _____ more than 5.

Operations and Algebraic Thinking I-45

OAI-46 Comparing to 5 and 10

 How many less than 10?

1.

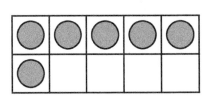

6 is _____ less than 10.

2.

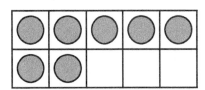

7 is _____ less than 10.

3.

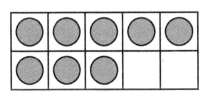

8 is _____ less than 10.

4.

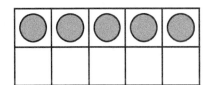

5 is _____ less than 10.

5.

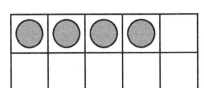

4 is _____ less than 10.

6.

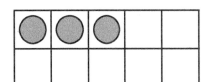

3 is _____ less than 10.

7.

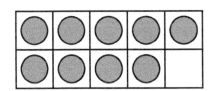

9 is _____ less than 10.

8.

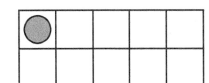

1 is _____ less than 10.

1	2	3	4	5	6	7	8	9	10
11	12	13	14	15	16	17	18	19	20

☐ How many more than 10?

9.
14 is __4__ more than 10.

10.
17 is ____ more than 10.

11.
19 is ____ more than 10.

12.
15 is ____ more than 10.

13.
11 is ____ more than 10.

14.
18 is ____ more than 10.

15.
16 is ____ more than 10.

16.
12 is ____ more than 10.

17.
13 is ____ more than 10.

18. BONUS
20 is _____ 10.

Operations and Algebraic Thinking 1-46

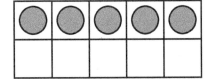 5

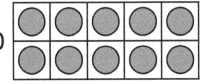 10

☐ Draw the dots.
☐ Fill in the blanks.

19.

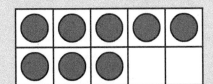 8

8 is __3__ more than 5.

8 is __2__ less than 10.

20.

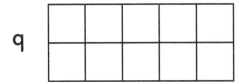 9

9 is ____ more than 5.

9 is ____ less than 10.

21.

 7

7 is ____ more than 5.

7 is ____ less than 10.

22.

 6

6 is ____ more than 5.

6 is ____ less than 10.

OAI-47 One More, One Less

☐ Add.

1. $3 + 2 = 5$ ○○○ ○○

so $4 + 2 = \underline{\ 6\ }$ ○○○● ○○

2. $7 + 3 = 10$ ○○○○○○○ ○○○

so $8 + 3 = \underline{\ \ \ \ }$ ○○○○○○○● ○○○

3. $8 + 2 = 10$ ○○○○○○○○ ○○

so $9 + 2 = \underline{\ \ \ \ }$ ○○○○○○○○● ○○

4. $6 + 4 = 10$ ○○○○○○ ○○○○

so $6 + 5 = \underline{\ \ \ \ }$ ○○○○○○ ○○○○●

5. $4 + 1 = 5$

so $4 + 2 = \underline{\ \ \ \ }$

6. $6 + 4 = 10$

so $7 + 4 = \underline{\ \ \ \ }$

7. $5 + 5 = \underline{\ \ \ \ }$

so $5 + 6 = \underline{\ \ \ \ }$

8. $3 + 2 = \underline{\ \ \ \ }$

so $3 + 3 = \underline{\ \ \ \ }$

☐ Take away I.

9.
7 + 3 = 10 ○ ○ ○ ○ ○ ○ ○   ○ ○ ○

so 7 + 2 = __9__ ○ ○ ○ ○ ○ ○ ○   ○ ○ ⊗

10.
3 + 2 = 5 ○ ○ ○   ○ ○

so 3 + 1 = ____ ○ ○ ○   ○ ⊗

11.
6 + 4 = 10 ○ ○ ○ ○ ○ ○   ○ ○ ○ ○

so 5 + 4 = ____ ○ ○ ○ ○ ○ ⊗   ○ ○ ○ ○

12.
4 + 1 = 5 ○ ○ ○ ○   ○

so 4 + 0 = ____ ○ ○ ○ ○   ⊗

13.
5 + 5 = 10

so 4 + 5 = ____

14.
2 + 3 = 5

so 2 + 2 = ____

15.
4 + 1 = 5

so 3 + 1 = ____

16.
5 + 5 = 10

so 5 + 4 = ____

☐ Add 1 or take away 1.

17.

$6 + 4 = 10$ ○ ○ ○ ○ ○ ○   ○ ○ ○ ○

so $6 + 3 =$ ___   ○ ○ ○ ○ ○ ○   ○ ○ ○ ⊗

18.

$6 + 4 = 10$ ○ ○ ○ ○ ○ ○   ○ ○ ○ ○

so $5 + 4 =$ ___   ○ ○ ○ ○ ⊗   ○ ○ ○ ○

19.

$7 + 3 = 10$ ○ ○ ○ ○ ○ ○ ○   ○ ○ ○

so $7 + 4 =$ ___   ○ ○ ○ ○ ○ ○ ○   ○ ○ ○ ●

20.

$7 + 3 = 10$

so $7 + 2 =$ ___

21.

$7 + 3 = 10$

so $6 + 3 =$ ___

22.

$5 + 5 = 10$

so $5 + 6 =$ ___

23.

$5 + 5 = 10$

so $4 + 5 =$ ___

24.

$8 + 2 = 10$

so $8 + 3 =$ ___

25.

$8 + 2 =$ ___

so $7 + 2 =$ ___

Operations and Algebraic Thinking 1-47

OAI-48 Pictures and Number Sentences

☐ Add the circles.

1.

_2_ white + _3_ black = _5_ in total

_3_ black + _2_ white = _5_ in total

2.

___ black + ___ white = ___ in total

___ white + ___ black = ___ in total

3.

___ white + ___ black = ___ in total

___ black + ___ white = ___ in total

4.

○ ○ ○ ○ ● ● ● ● ●

___ black + ___ white = ___ in total

___ white + ___ black = ___ in total

⬜ Add or subtract the squares.

5.

■ ■ □ □ □ □ □

___ black + ___ white = ___ in total

___ white + ___ black = ___ in total

___ squares − ___ black = ___ white

___ squares − ___ white = ___ black

6.

□ □ □ ■ ■ ■ ■ ■

___ black + ___ white = ___ in total

___ white + ___ black = ___ in total

___ squares − ___ black = ___ white

___ squares − ___ white = ___ black

7.

□ □ □ □ ■ ■ ■ ■ ■ ■

___ black + ___ white = ___ in total

___ white + ___ black = ___ in total

___ squares − ___ black = ___ white

___ squares − ___ white = ___ black

Operations and Algebraic Thinking 1-48

☐ Write 2 addition sentences for the picture.
☐ Write 2 subtraction sentences for the picture.

8.

$4 + 1 = 5$ $1 + 4 = 5$

$5 - 4 = 1$ $5 - 1 = 4$

9.

_____   _____

_____   _____

10.

_____   _____

_____   _____

11.

_____   _____

_____   _____

☐ Write 4 number sentences for the picture.

12.

[■][■][■][□][□][□][□]

$\underline{\quad 3 \quad} + \underline{\quad 4 \quad} = \underline{\quad 7 \quad}$

$\underline{\quad 4 \quad} + \underline{\quad 3 \quad} = \underline{\quad 7 \quad}$

$\underline{\quad 7 \quad} - \underline{\quad 4 \quad} = \underline{\quad 3 \quad}$

$\underline{\quad 7 \quad} - \underline{\quad 3 \quad} = \underline{\quad 4 \quad}$

13.

$$\begin{array}{r} 2 \\ + \ 4 \\ \hline 6 \end{array}$$

[■]
[■]
[□]
[□]
[□]
[□]

$$\begin{array}{r} 6 \\ - \ 4 \\ \hline 2 \end{array}$$

$$\begin{array}{r} 4 \\ + \ 2 \\ \hline 6 \end{array}$$

$$\begin{array}{r} 6 \\ - \ 2 \\ \hline 4 \end{array}$$

14.

[■][■][□][□][□][□][□]

$\underline{\qquad} + \underline{\qquad} = \underline{\qquad}$

$\underline{\qquad} + \underline{\qquad} = \underline{\qquad}$

$\underline{\qquad} - \underline{\qquad} = \underline{\qquad}$

$\underline{\qquad} - \underline{\qquad} = \underline{\qquad}$

15. BONUS

$$\begin{array}{r} 6 \\ + \ 1 \\ \hline 7 \end{array}$$

[□]
[□]
[□]
[□]
[□]
[□]
[■]

$$\begin{array}{r} 7 \\ - \ 1 \\ \hline 6 \end{array}$$

$$+ \underline{\qquad}$$

$$- \underline{\qquad}$$

16.

[■][□][□][□][□][□]

$\underline{\hspace{6cm}}$

$\underline{\hspace{6cm}}$

$\underline{\hspace{6cm}}$

$\underline{\hspace{6cm}}$

Operations and Algebraic Thinking 1-48

OAI-49 More Pictures and Number Sentences

☐ Add or subtract.

1.

____ dogs + ____ cats = ____ pets

____ cats + ____ dogs = ____ pets

____ pets − ____ dogs = ____ cats

____ pets − ____ cats = ____ dogs

2.

____ bunnies + ____ hamsters = ____ pets

____ hamsters + ____ bunnies = ____ pets

____ pets − ____ bunnies = ____ hamsters

____ pets − ____ hamsters = ____ bunnies

◻ Write 4 number sentences for the picture.

3.

| 2 + 5 = 7 | 5 + 2 = 7 |
| 7 − 5 = 2 | 7 − 2 = 5 |

4.

_____   _____

_____   _____

◻ Write 4 number sentences.

5.

4 cups   3 plates

_____   _____

_____   _____

6.

5 cars   2 vans

_____   _____

_____   _____

⬜ How many animals?

7.
2 cats   3 dogs   4 rabbits

___ + ___ + ___ = ___

8.
2 turtles   3 frogs   1 fish

___ + ___ + ___ = ___

9.
2 goats   3 cows   3 pigs

___ + ___ + ___ = ___

10.
1 lion   5 tigers   3 bears

___ + ___ + ___ = ___

11. BONUS

3 cats   2 dogs   4 rabbits

How many animals?

___ + ___ + ___ = ___

2 rabbits hop away.

How many animals are there now?

___ – ___ = ___

OAI-50 Comparing Numbers Using Pictures

☐ Circle the **extra** ⬤ to find how many more.

☐ Fill in the blanks.

1.

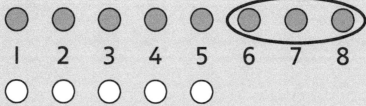

There are __8__ ⬤. There are __5__ ◯.

There are __3__ more ⬤ than ◯.

2.

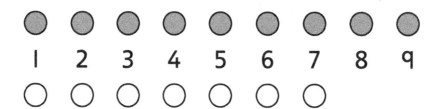

There are ____ ⬤. There are ____ ◯.

There are ____ more ⬤ than ◯.

3.

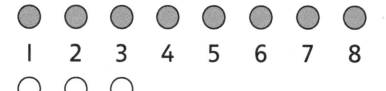

There are ____ ⬤. There are ____ ◯.

There are ____ more ⬤ than ◯.

☐ Circle the extra ○.
☐ Fill in the blanks.

4.

○ ○ ○ ○ ○ ○ ○
1 2 3 4 5 6 7
● ● ●

There are ____ ○. There are ____ ●.

There are ____ more ○ than ●.

5.

● ● ● ● ● ● ●
1 2 3 4 5 6 7 8
○ ○ ○ ○ ○ ○ ○ ○

There are ____ ○. There are ____ ●.

There are ____ more ○ than ●.

6.

○ ○ ○ ○ ○ ○ ○ ○ ○
1 2 3 4 5 6 7 8 9
● ● ● ●

There are ____ ○. There are ____ ●.

There are ____ more ○ than ●.

☐ Circle the extra ●.
☐ Fill in the blanks.

7.

● ● ● ● ● ●
1 2 3 4 5 6
○ ○ ○ ○ ○

There are ____ ●. There are ____ ○.
There are ____ more ● than ○.

8.

● ● ● ● ● ● ● ● ●
1 2 3 4 5 6 7 8 9
○ ○ ○ ○ ○ ○

There are ____ ●. There are ____ ○.
There are ____ more ● than ○.

9.

○ ○
1 2 3 4 5 6 7
● ● ● ● ● ● ●

There are ____ ●. There are ____ ○.
There are ____ more ● than ○.

Operations and Algebraic Thinking 1-50

Draw a picture to find the answer.

Use ⬤ and ◯.

10.

5 cats ⬤ ⬤ ⬤ ⬤ ⬤

4 dogs ◯ ◯ ◯ ◯

How many more cats? __1__

11.

4 cats

6 dogs

How many more dogs? ____

12.

6 cats

3 dogs

How many more cats? ____

13.

2 cats

7 dogs

How many more dogs? ____

OAI-51 More Addition Word Problems

☐ Draw circles to show the numbers.
☐ Write the number sentence.
☐ Fill in the answer.

1.

There are 3 cats. ● ● ●

There are 4 dogs. ○ ○ ○ ○

There are __7__ animals altogether.

$$\begin{array}{r} 3 \\ +\ 4 \\ \hline 7 \end{array}$$

2.

There are 6 yellow crayons.

There are 5 blue crayons.

There are ____ crayons in total.

$$+ \ \square$$

3.

Zara has 2 big toys.

She has 8 small toys.

Zara has ____ toys in total.

$$+ \ \square$$

4.

John has 7 shirts.

He has 6 sweaters.

John has ____ tops altogether.

$$+ \ \square$$

⬜ Draw circles to show the numbers.
⬜ Write the number sentence.
⬜ Fill in the answer.

5.

5 birds are in a tree.

3 birds join them.

There are ____ birds in the tree.

$+$ ☐
☐
☐

6.

4 frogs are in a pond.

2 frogs join them.

There are ____ frogs in the pond.

$+$ ☐
☐
☐

7.

6 adults are in a pool.

3 children jump in.

There are ____ people in the pool.

$+$ ☐
☐
☐

8.

Ken has 3 dimes.

Amy has 4 dimes.

They have ____ dimes altogether.

$+$ ☐
☐
☐

☐ Write the number sentence in 2 ways.
☐ Fill in the answer.

9.

Kim has 5 balls.

Ron has 3 balls.

They have ____ balls altogether.

$$\square + \square = \square$$

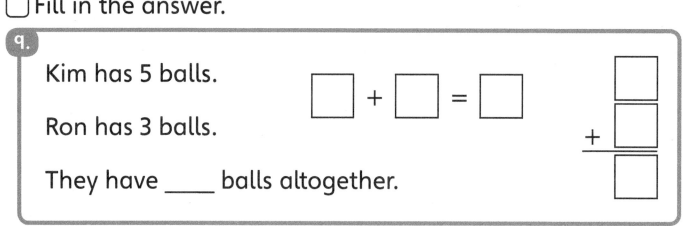

10.

Tess has 3 pens.

Ben has 2 pens.

They have ____ pens in all.

$$\square + \square = \square$$

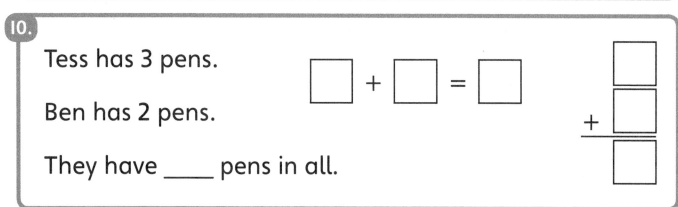

11.

Raj has 4 hats.

Mary has 3 hats.

They have ____ hats in total.

$$\square + \square = \square$$

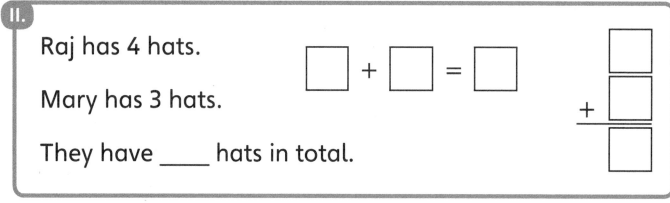

12.

Ava has 2 new books.

She has 3 old books.

Ava has ____ books in total.

$$\square + \square = \square$$

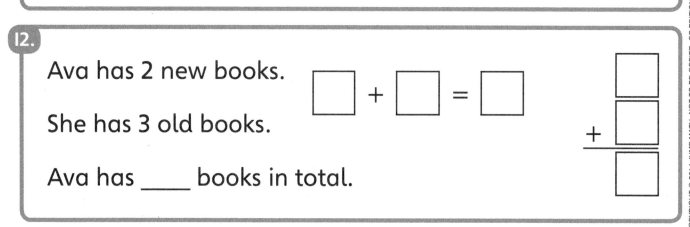

Operations and Algebraic Thinking 1-51

OAI-52 More Subtraction Word Problems

☐ Draw circles and cross out to subtract.
☐ Write the subtraction sentence.
☐ Fill in the answer.

1.
Jason has 8 crayons.   ⊗ ⊗ ⊗ ◯ ◯ ◯ ◯ ◯

He gives 3 to his sister.

Jason has __5__ crayons left.

$$\begin{array}{r} 8 \\ -\ 3 \\ \hline 5 \end{array}$$

2.
Helen has 4 pencils.

She loses 1 of them.

Helen has ____ pencils left.

$$\begin{array}{r} \square \\ -\ \square \\ \hline \square \end{array}$$

3.
Lily has 6 marbles.

She gives 2 to Alex.

Lily has ____ marbles left.

$$\begin{array}{r} \square \\ -\ \square \\ \hline \square \end{array}$$

4.
Sal has 5 toy cars.

His teacher takes 3 of them.

Now Sal has ____ toy cars.

$$\begin{array}{r} \square \\ -\ \square \\ \hline \square \end{array}$$

☐ Draw circles and cross out to subtract.
☐ Write the subtraction sentence.
☐ Fill in the answer.

5.

5 rabbits are on the grass.

2 of them hop away.

There are _____ rabbits on the grass.

$$\begin{array}{r}\boxed{}\\[2pt]-\boxed{}\\[2pt]\hline\boxed{}\end{array}$$

6.

6 frogs are on a log.

4 frogs hop off.

Now _____ frogs are on the log.

$$\begin{array}{r}\boxed{}\\[2pt]-\boxed{}\\[2pt]\hline\boxed{}\end{array}$$

7.

6 children play tag.

3 go home.

Now _____ children are playing tag.

$$\begin{array}{r}\boxed{}\\[2pt]-\boxed{}\\[2pt]\hline\boxed{}\end{array}$$

8.

Clara has 5 grapes.

She eats 3 of them.

Clara has _____ grapes left.

$$\begin{array}{r}\boxed{}\\[2pt]-\boxed{}\\[2pt]\hline\boxed{}\end{array}$$

Operations and Algebraic Thinking 1-52

☐ Write the number sentence in 2 ways.

☐ Fill in the answer.

9.

Fred has 5 crayons.

He uses up 4 of them.

Now Fred has ____ crayon.

☐ – ☐ = ☐

☐
– ☐
―――
☐

10.

Rani has 4 crackers.

She eats I cracker.

Rani has ____ crackers left.

☐ – ☐ = ☐

☐
– ☐
―――
☐

11.

5 bears are in a cave.

3 bears leave.

There are ____ bears in the cave.

☐ – ☐ = ☐

☐
– ☐
―――
☐

12.

6 kites fly in the sky.

4 of them fall down.

There are ____ kites flying.

☐ – ☐ = ☐

☐
– ☐
―――
☐

OAI-53 Addition and Subtraction Word Problems

☐ Draw a picture to show the numbers.
☐ Write the number sentence.
   Remember to write the + sign.
☐ Fill in the answer.

1.

There are 3 cats. ○ ○ ○

There are 4 dogs. ○ ○ ○ ○

There are ____ animals.

$$\begin{array}{r} 3 \\ + \ 4 \\ \hline 7 \end{array}$$

2.

4 birds are in a tree.

3 birds are on the ground.

There are ____ birds in total.

3.

Kim has 2 balls.

Tom has 4 balls.

They have ____ balls in total.

4.

4 books are on a table.

5 books are on a shelf.

There are ____ books in total.

⬜ Draw a picture to show the numbers.

⬜ Write the number sentence.
   Remember to write the − sign.

⬜ Fill in the answer.

5.

Don has 5 apples.

He gives Hanna 3 apples.

Now Don has ____ apples.

$$\frac{\boxed{}}{\boxed{}}\;\boxed{}$$

6.

Mandy has 6 grapes.

She eats 4 grapes.

Mandy has ____ grapes left.

$$\frac{\boxed{}}{\boxed{}}\;\boxed{}$$

7.

5 rabbits are on the grass.

2 of them hop away.

Now ____ rabbits are on the grass.

$$\frac{\boxed{}}{\boxed{}}\;\boxed{}$$

8.

5 cars are on the street.

3 of them drive away.

There are ____ cars on the street.

$$\frac{\boxed{}}{\boxed{}}\;\boxed{}$$

☐ Draw a picture to show the numbers.
☐ Write the number sentence. Include the + or − sign.
☐ Fill in the answer.

9.

Jen has 5 balls.

Mark has 3 balls.

They have ____ balls in total.

10.

Ben has 4 balls.

He gives 3 balls away.

Ben has ____ balls left.

11.

Emma has 3 balls.

She loses 2 of them.

She has ____ ball left.

12.

Kathy has 5 balls.

Sam has 1 ball.

They have ____ balls altogether.

☐ Draw a picture to show the numbers.
☐ Write a number sentence.
☐ Fill in the answer.

13.

4 cats are in a basket.

3 cats climb in.

There are ____ cats in the basket.

14.

6 cats are in a basket.

4 cats climb out.

There are ____ cats in the basket.

15.

A dog has 3 treats.

He eats 1 treat.

The dog has ____ treats left.

16.

6 dogs are in the park.

4 dogs join them.

There are ____ dogs in the park.